C000075841

Battle Orders • 30

Mobile Strike Forces
in Vietnam 1966–70

Gordon L Rottman

Consultant Editor Dr Duncan Anderson • *Series editors* Marcus Cowper and Nikolai Bogdanovic

First published in Great Britain in 2007 by Osprey Publishing
Midland House, West Way, Botley, Oxford OX2 0PH, United Kingdom
443 Park Avenue South, New York, NY 10016, USA
Email: info@ospreypublishing.com

ISBN 978 184603 139 7

Editorial by Ilios Publishing, Oxford, UK (www.iliospublishing.com)
Page layout by Boundford.com, Huntingdon. UK
Index by Glyn Sutcliffe
Typeset in GillSans and Stone Serif
Originated by United Graphics, Singapore
Printed in China through Bookbuilders

07 08 09 10 11   10 9 8 7 6 5 4 3 2 1

A CIP catalog record for this book is available from the British Library.

For a catalog of all books published by Osprey Military and Aviation please contact:

Osprey Direct USA, c/o Random House Distribution Center, 400 Hahn Rd,
Westminster, MD 21157 USA
E-mail: info@ospreydirect.com

Osprey Direct UK, P.O. Box 140, Wellingborough, Northants, NN8 2FA, UK
E-mail: info@ospreydirect.co.uk

www.ospreypublishing.com

Image credits

The photographic images that appear in this work were obtained
from US government sources, unless otherwise stated.

Author's note

The author is deeply indebted to Steve Sherman of RADIX Press
without whose assistance and research materials this book would
not have been possible.

Key to military symbols

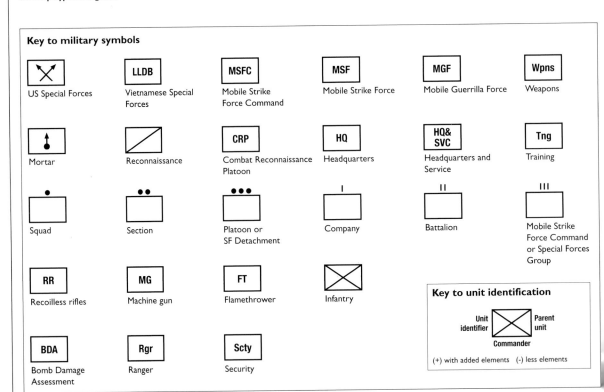

Contents

Introduction

The black and white flag of the 4th Battalion, II Corps MIKE Force. It displays the old MIKE Force patch on the left and the full-color 2d MSFC patch to the right.

The US Army Special Forces (USSF), also known as the "Green Berets," performed a wide variety of missions in Vietnam, many of them unique and never since duplicated. The primary mission was to advise the Civilian Irregular Defense Group (CIDG – pronounced "sidge" – the Vietnamese name being Luc-Luong Biet Kich). This was a paramilitary counterinsurgency force comprising indigenous minorities who were essentially civilian employees of the US Army; the CIDG was not a component of the Army of the Republic of Vietnam (ARVN). The USSF trained, armed, equipped, uniformed, paid, and otherwise supported the CIDG. The Vietnamese Airborne Special Forces Command, or Nhay-Du Luc-Luong Dac-Biet (LLDB), held actual command authority over the CIDG and the USSF served as advisors, although in reality USSF ran the entire operation because of the control it maintained over resources. The Camp Strike Forces (CSFs) operated from fortified camps established in remote areas to protect local villages from Viet Cong (VC) exploitation, conducted border surveillance, infiltration interdiction, raids, and reconnaissance-in-force in their assigned tactical areas of responsibility (TAORs). The CSFs were battalion-size units recruited mostly from local natives signed up to defend their homes and families. Their arms, level of training, and state of mind did not make them suited for long-duration operations outside of their home areas.

Over 80 camps were in operation at the height of the CIDG program. Scores more had been opened, closed, or relocated between 1962 and 1970. They were often attacked by the VC and North Vietnamese Army (NVA). Only seven camps were actually overrun between 1963 and 1968, although others came close to falling during bitter battles. Other camp attacks developed into prolonged sieges. Many camps successfully fought off their attackers, but in some instances outside reinforcements or relief forces were necessary. There were times when such forces were not available as nearby Free World units were engaged or were not willing to commit to risky camp relief operations. Such support was occasionally denied by the US Army, Marines, or ARVN for various reasons, political or tactical.

To ensure some form of reinforcement was immediately available USSF concluded that dedicated reaction forces were necessary. Additionally, reaction forces under the direct command and leadership of USSF would be more responsive and flexible than those provided by other forces.

From 1964 a number of small reaction forces were raised for local use, such as Eagle Flights. In 1966 5th Special Forces Group (Airborne)[1] directed that five Mobile Strike (MIKE) Forces be established – one in each of the four corps tactical zones (CTZs) and a fifth for countrywide use by the 5th SFGA Headquarters. These units were to be manned by especially recruited and trained CIDG troops provided with parachute and airmobile training. They were initially of battalion size and led by a USSF A-team, usually two officers

---

1 The 5th SFGA assumed command of all USSF activities in Vietnam on October 1, 1965 taking over from a provisional command, US Army Special Forces, Vietnam.

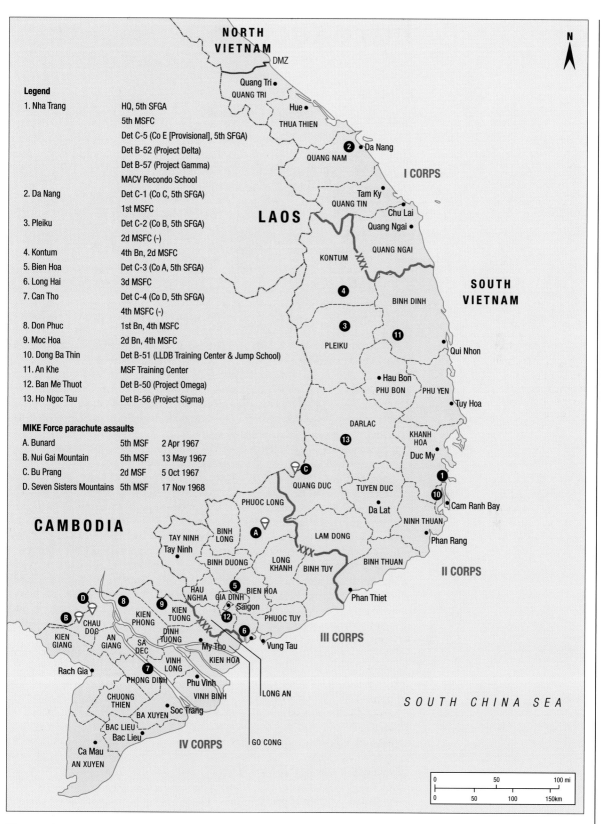

N

This map shows the MIKE Force reconnaissance project, 5th SFGA command locations, and the locations of MIKE Force parachute assaults during the war. Also shown are the administrative provinces of the country, and the four Corps Tactical Zones.

Off-duty members of the 5th MIKE Force in their base camp club with LTC Martha Reye (Army Reserve Nurse Corps). "Maggie," as she was known to Special Forces soldiers, toured Vietnam every year, visiting almost every SF camp and installation. (Frank Nicholas)

and ten NCOs. Until 1968 there were no LLDB assigned, being totally under American command.

The MIKE Forces quickly grew in size to reach brigade strength with two to five battalions apiece and an A-team leading each. They were under the tactical command of a B-team. Besides reinforcing and relieving endangered camps, they secured sites where camps were under construction and while the CSF was being recruited and trained. They also conducted large-scale, independent offensive operations as their level of experience and confidence progressed. The MIKE Forces became highly capable units led by a small number of Americans with USSF NCOs commanding companies and platoons. Included in these operations were the short-lived Mobile Guerrilla Forces (MGFs). These were company-size unconventional warfare units conducting missions in remote enemy-controlled areas using the enemy's guerrilla methods.

USSF also ran several special reconnaissance projects tasked with collecting information on enemy activities in their base areas and on infiltration trails. These "Greek-letter" projects executed operational-level missions providing higher commands with valuable intelligence. The highly classified Military Assistance Command, Vietnam–Studies and Observation Group (MACV-SOG) was a joint unconventional special operations task force tasked with conducting strategic and operational reconnaissance missions mainly in Laos and Cambodia. While most SOG reconnaissance personnel were Special Forces, MACV-SOG itself was not a USSF unit and is therefore beyond the remit of this book.

A Montagnard striker ensemble play their traditional brass gongs at a victory celebration.

Combat mission

MIKE Forces and their predecessors were primarily organized to serve as reaction forces to reinforce or otherwise aid remote CIDG camps under or in danger of attack. Prior to 1964 there were no reaction forces under USSF command. The camps were manned by often understrength, lightly armed, moderately trained self-defense forces. They were recruited locally and their degree of motivation varied. The ARVN viewed these camps as being under US control, even though they were ostensibly under the command of the LLDB. Local ARVN commanders were reluctant to commit forces to relieve or reinforce these camps. The same applied to the local provincial and district chiefs who seldom committed their Provincial or Popular Force units, which were also locally recruited and poorly trained and armed. Often they lacked the mobility to conduct a relief. There was also a very real concern that any ground relief force would be ambushed en route. US Army and Marine units too proved to be reluctant to respond to endangered camps. While US units possessed the airmobility necessary to rapidly respond, they had little inclination to conduct risky, usually at night, relief operations for what they viewed as "Special Forces-owned" camps not under their operational control.

It was the almost-successful July 1964 VC attack on Nam Dong Camp that accelerated the organization of USSF-controlled reaction forces. CPT (later MG) David E. Watts related the sequence of events leading to the formation of the first reaction force:

> In the following days we all devoted much analysis to the Nam Dong episode. As professional soldiers we knew that every combat structure must have some kind of "reserve" and that that we – and I CTZ LLDB – had none. I believe that realization compelled us to begin thinking "Reaction Force." Our little B-team had no inherent power and no power unit at our disposal. We had to have some "organic power" that could be organized and equipped to fight offensively. Too, it had to be mobile (preferably by air). ARVN had such units called Airborne Rangers. But they belonged to the ARVN and would not be expended to "save" a CIDG camp. Thus it became clear that we would have to create our own force.[2]

The formation of the company-size I CTZ Nung Reaction Force was accomplished with a degree of deception being established as though a new CIDG camp was being built and manned. Nung mercenaries were recruited from Saigon as they already had a reputation of loyalty to USSF, having been used as bodyguards, and they had a soldierly reputation. However, they were accused of being a mafia-like organization, and were not always in the best physical shape. Besides serving as mobile reaction forces, they were soon deployed to conduct raids and recovery operations.

In II CTZ a second effort to create a reaction force developed. The Eagle Flight Detachment was formed in October 1964 under B-210, 1st SFGA as directed by C-2. A-311A (split A-team) at Pleiku was responsible for the Eagle Flight. It consisted of two platoons of selected Rhade Montagnard strikers trained in airmobile operations, small-unit tactics, and weapons. The Eagle Flight was not a USSF-developed concept, but was created in early 1963 by US advisors with ARVN units.

---

2 From *After-Action Reports: I CTZ MIKE Force* (RADIX Associates, Houston, TX).

The distribution of the major ethnic groups in the Republic of Vietnam. Nungs are not depicted, as they lived in scattered settlements along the western border of the Central Highlands, or had fled North Vietnam and had settled in cities.

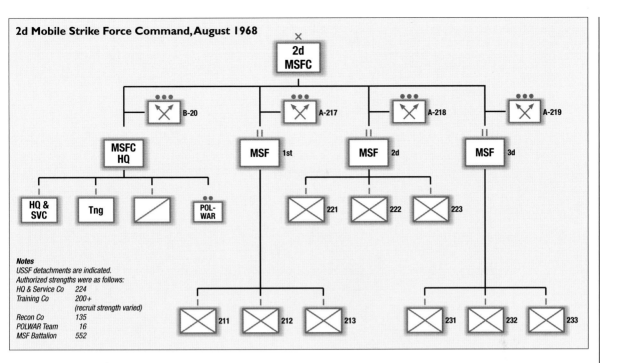

2d Mobile Strike Force Command, August 1968

2d MSFC

B-20 — MSFC HQ — HQ & SVC | Tng | | POL-WAR

A-217 — MSF 1st — 221 | 222 | 223

A-218 — MSF 2d

A-219 — MSF 3d — 231 | 232 | 233

211 | 212 | 213

Notes
USSF detachments are indicated.
Authorized strengths were as follows:

HQ & Service Co	224
Training Co	200+
	(recruit strength varied)
Recon Co	135
POLWAR Team	16
MSF Battalion	552

The Eagle Flight was on 24-hour alert for helicopter insertion to reinforce or rescue separated personnel undertaking CSF operations or downed aircrewmen. They were well equipped with demolitions to destroy any downed aircraft. These were known as Angel Flight missions. Eagle Flight operations proved highly successful because of the flexibility under which they operated. The helicopters were provided by the Army's 52d Aviation Battalion (Combat). In January 1965 the Eagle Flight was moved to Bam Me Thuot under A-334B assigned to B-21. There it was given the mission of securing the 52d Aviation Battalion's airfield and was known as the Holloway Army Airfield Force (HAAF). It was further used for diversions, flank security, reconnaissance, target acquisition, and bomb damage assessment (BDA) in support of other CIDG operations. The small unit was conducting a large number of short-term missions. In November 1965, now under A-219, it was planned to absorb the Eagle Flight into the II CTZ MIKE Force. In December the Eagle Flight was given parachute ground training, but made no jumps owing to a lack of jump pay funds. It was soon integrated into the MIKE Force as its combat reconnaissance platoon (CRP). As such it continued to employ Eagle Flight airmobile techniques. It is often said that the II CTZ MIKE Force was formed from the

Montagnard strikers of the 5th MSF butcher a water buffalo for a "jug and bracket" ceremony for USSF A-503 members being made honorary tribal members. (Scott Whitting)

9

Eagle Flight, but the success of the Eagle Flight led to the realization that a larger reaction force would be valuable.

The original combat mission of the battalion-size MIKE Force officially described it as a "multi-purpose reaction force located in each of the four Corps areas, and an additional unit to be located at Nha Trang." Its mission was:

a. Constitute a C-team reserve.
b. Conduct raids, ambushes, and combat patrols.
c. Be prepared to reinforce CIDG camps under attack.
d. Conduct search and secure operations.
e. Conduct small-scale conventional combat operations.

Their assignment was described as being:

> based upon geographic areas as directed by Headquarters, 5th SFGA. It is anticipated that each force will operate in its own respective corps area, however, CO, 5th SFGA is authorized to employ each unit anywhere in the Republic of South Vietnam according to the tactical situation, provided necessary coordination with LLDB High Command and MACV Headquarters can be made. Normally, each C detachment commander will employ this reaction force as a reserve in its Corps Area. CO, 5th SFGA has the capability to reinforce any Corps Area when the situation threatens.

The C-team reserve provided a unit the C-team commander could commit when and where needed within the CTZ. While a C-team commander had perhaps a dozen or more battalion-size CSFs available, these were static local forces tied to their base camp and responsible for securing area villages and interdicting enemy infiltration through their assigned TAOR. The troops were recruited locally with the understanding that they would remain in the area defending their homes. They were not trained, equipped, or motivated to deploy to other areas, which would have left their TAOR unsecured.

Raids, ambushes, and combat patrols were routine operations expected of any CIDG unit. Search and secure operations were usually longer duration missions in which a unit conducted sweeps of an area and could secure objectives, such as villages, to prevent their exploitation by the enemy. The ability to conduct small-scale conventional combat operations gave the C-team the ability to conduct offensive missions in areas outside of the CSF TAORs, to augment camp operations, or to support other Free World forces.

One of the most important missions, though, was to support CIDG camps in danger of or under attack. This reduced the necessity to rely on support from other Free World forces, which was not always forthcoming. Another mission not listed was to secure construction sites for future camps, defend them, and patrol the surrounding area while the local CSF was recruited and trained. They also conducted area assessments of proposed camp sites, moving into and reconnoitering the surrounding area while engineers surveyed the site. Recovery missions were also frequently conducted to recover the remains of aircrew, radios, and equipment from downed aircraft. They sometimes provided security for classified Air Force reconnaissance drone recovery operations. Security and escort missions were conducted to return refugees to their villages after fleeing the VC or to relocate civilians to secure areas. They also sometimes escorted truck convoys near their base camp. MIKE Force medical personnel would also provide minor assistance to villagers.

Mobile strike force (MSF) missions were economy-of-force operations. They were of low cost to establish, maintain, and operate when compared to those of conventional US, ARVN, or other Free World forces. Even given their modest firepower and strength, they were effective owing to the leadership and experience of the USSF.

By mid-1967 there were 19 MSF companies. The expansion of the MIKE Forces to brigades in late 1968 greatly enhanced their capabilities allowing large-scale or multiple missions to be conducted. They also permitted battalions to rest and recover after prolonged missions, or rebuild and retrain after a mauling while other battalions continued operations. More battalion-size operations began to be conducted. Previously the various companies conducted mostly independent operations.

The MIKE Forces were parachute qualified and this capability allowed them to be parachuted in to commence offensive operations, reinforce an endangered camp, or secure the site of a future camp. Some felt the need for parachute troops was negated by the use of helicopters. However, parachute insertion from fixed-wing transports offered several advantages. It required a large number of helicopters and multiple lifts to insert a battalion, as there were seldom enough helicopters available to conduct a single lift – nor were landing zones large enough to land such a large force. To deliver a 120-man company required about 18 helicopter sorties or two C-130 transports. Helicopters were relatively short ranged and MIKE Forces often operated in remote areas some distance from launch bases, meaning that the round trips and refueling stops were time-consuming. It might require several hours to deliver the entire force onto a landing zone. This meant the first lift was vulnerable while awaiting the rest of the force, and it would be sometime before the force was built up and departed the LZ. This delay allowed the VC to either withdraw from the area or mass for a counterattack. Transports were not limited by the range and their use freed helicopters to support other operations. Parachute training also instilled self-confidence, aggressiveness, and an elite standing, all of which improved motivation.

It must be remembered that the MIKE Forces, while effective units, were paramilitary forces manned by irregular volunteers; the use of the term "mercenaries" was discouraged. There were limitations to their employment which had to be considered. This excerpt from the 2d MSFC (Mobile Strike Force Command) October 1968 *Monthly Operational Summary* demonstrates these limitations:

E. Utilization of the Mobile Strike Force. Since April 1968, the 2d MSFC has been utilized continuously on 30-day operations with minimum time allowed for standdown. As a result of this practice indigenous personnel have not had sufficient time to recover, both physically and mentally, before they find themselves back in the field. With little time to settle personal matters and visit their families, some of the indigenous personnel have resorted to AWOL and desertion measures. The primary mission of the 2d MSFC is to constitute a reaction force for A detachments [camps] within II CTZ. It is significant that during the battle of Duc Lap [August 23–25, 1968] it was purely a matter of chance that sufficient companies were in transit to a new AO [area of operations] and were able to be diverted into Duc Lap. Due to operational commitments there is usually only one company available for deployment. This would hardly suffice to relieve any camp within II CTZ.

F. AWOL and desertion. As of 30 April 1968, the indigenous strength of the 2d MSFC was 1,656. As of October our indigenous strength was 1,598. Between April and October we trained 649 replacements for the command. This represents a net loss of 707 individuals. Of these only 32 were killed in action. It must be remembered that the CIDG soldiers can quit at any time. It must also be remembered that simple things like time to visit their families and the equipment they take to the field are factors of prime importance in maintaining the morale of indigenous soldiers. When one is dealing with Montagnards another

Nungs of Mobile Guerrilla Force (A-113) prepare to load up for an extended operation in the Gia Vuc area of operations. The company carried one 60mm M19 mortar and one 57mm M18A1 recoilless rifle. (Virgil R. Carter)

factor enters the picture, and that is that many of the highland tribes are a matriarchal society. This is particularly true of the Rhade and Jarai, and the majority of this command is from these tribes. When a soldier's family tires of not seeing him they will bring pressure upon him to quit the CIDG and in the majority of cases he will comply. Therefore the continuous 30-day operations in the field, without sufficient time allotted for standdown and refitting, contribute directly to the loss of strength within this command. The above problems deserve serious consideration, especially if this command is to fulfill the mission with which we have been entrusted.

As the MIKE Forces evolved, their mission grew more complex and refined. In 1968 the MSFC mission statement was as follows:

1. General:
a. The mission of the MSFC B detachment is to exercise joint command and control of the MSFC in conjunction with the assigned LLDB detachment.
b. The B detachment will be under the command and control of the CO, 5th SFGA company [C detachment] responsible for the CTZ.

The Da Nang base of the I CTZ MIKE Force with the Da Nang River in the background. The striker barracks are to the left and the row extends far off camera. The C Company C-team (C-1) headquarters and other facilities are in the center and right. (Virgil R. Carter)

A typical striker "hootch" in the field, a poncho strung up for protection from the rain and sun, and a nylon hammock. This was a much more comfortable arrangement than the conventional US practice of sleeping on the ground and reduced bug infestation. Of course when contact was imminent hootches were not erected. (Jess Smetherman)

c. The B detachment will be responsible for the operation of the MSFC base camp and the operation of mission support sites as assigned by the company CO.

2. Mobile Strike Force Command:

a. Mission:

    (1) Constitutes the CTZ reserve ready reaction force for CIDG camps.

    (2) Conduct long-range reconnaissance and support of the senior US command within the CTZ.

    (3) Conduct mobile guerrilla type operations.

    (4) Conduct combat operations to relieve any pressure on CIDG camps.

    (5) Reinforce CIDG camp defense systems when attack is imminent.

    (6) Reinforce CIDG camps under attack.

    (7) Conduct battalion-size small-scale conventional combat operations.

A II CTZ MIKE Force patrol base. The poncho hootches were erected in an irregular layout. An AN/PRC-25 radio with the long whip antenna sits beside the striker in the foreground. (Jess Smetherman)

(8) Conduct raids, ambushes, combat patrols, and search and clear operations in designated areas.

(9) Constitute a reaction and exploitation force responsive to hard intelligence produced by organic reconnaissance assets.

(10) Conduct other missions as assigned by CO, LLDB High Command and CO, 5th SFGA.

b. Capabilities:

(1) To conduct small-scale conventional type operations.

(2) To provide reconnaissance teams to collect intelligence information in denied areas.

(3) To provide special action platoons to engage limited targets of opportunity.

(4) To conduct separate mobile guerrilla operations for durations up to 30 days in enemy controlled areas.

(5) To participate in heliborne exploitation force operations.

(6) To act as an exploitation force reacting to hard intelligence generated by reconnaissance.

(7) To be inserted into an AO by helicopter, parachute assault, or overland for the purpose of conducting combat operations.

(8) To conduct political warfare[3] activities in support of assigned missions.

Mobile Guerrilla Force mission

Unconventional warfare (guerrilla warfare) pits large, well-equipped conventional maneuver and security forces against a small, lightly equipped irregular force. The conventional government forces defend or strive to defend major population and commercial centers, secure lines-of-communications and economic resources, and deny the guerrillas access to sympathetic segments of the population. This allows the more agile and flexible guerrillas, capable of blending into the population, to initiate actions against cumbersome government forces tied to defensive installations and their logistical tail, to initiate action when and where they please, and when the situation is to their advantage. Offensive operations by government troops are usually responses to guerrilla activity, with the guerrillas avoiding contact and melting away. They hold nothing, but manage to gain support from at least a portion of the population. Conventional forces often lash out at thin air.

In an effort to take the war to the enemy and turn his successful techniques against him, the MGF concept was developed by Colonel Francis J. Kelly in late 1966. The idea was to covertly infiltrate a light but well-armed force into a VC-controlled area, in which they felt secure and operated bases. To an extent this tied the VC to fixed installations as they had to protect their own logistics centers. Either there had never been a government presence in these areas, or they had been forced out long before. Special Forces had its roots in guerrilla warfare. They were to establish contact with and cultivate guerrilla operations in communist-occupied countries in the event of a war in Europe. When the need arose for counter-guerrilla forces in Vietnam, Special Forces was called. It was natural that Special Forces would use guerrilla techniques against the enemies.

The mission of the MGFs was "To infiltrate into the area of operations and conduct border surveillance, interdict infiltration routes, and conduct guerrilla-type operations against known VC installations." Infiltration, reconnaissance, operations, and exfiltration would be executed clandestinely.

The MGF was a three-platoon company augmented by a small reconnaissance platoon led by a USSF A-team. No LLDB were involved. The

---

3 "Political warfare" comprised "white" psychological operations (truthful, factual information), morale building, medical aid, economic aid (distribution of farm tools, seed, building materials, etc.), and assorted other efforts to counter VC political activity.

Company guidons of the 5th MSF are presented during an awards ceremony in its Nha Trang base.

missions were supposed to be of 30–60 days' duration, but the reality was that they could seldom remain on the ground this long because of the difficulties of resupply, enemy pressure once discovered, and deteriorating physical condition. Two MGFs were formed in each corps area under the direct control of the C-team commander and sometimes attached to the MSF for support.

Special reconnaissance mission

From 1965 US divisions and separate brigades were assigned long-range reconnaissance companies and detachments, respectively. Long Range Patrol (LRP) units, redesignated "Ranger" in 1969, comprised small reconnaissance teams tasked with insertion within their parent unit's AO to covertly search for and report the locations and activities of enemy forces. These were tactical reconnaissance missions. In order to collect operational intelligence in remote areas of South Vietnam, special reconnaissance units were directed to be established by Military Assistance Command, Vietnam (MACV) under USSF, in what are called the "Greek letter" projects.

This resulted in the establishment of Projects DELTA, SIGMA, and OMEGA. Their multi-faceted missions included operational and strategic reconnaissance into long-established VC base areas and sanctuaries to direct air strikes on discovered targets; conduct bomb damage assessments and small-scale reconnaissance-in-force and hunter-killer operations; capture VC/NVA prisoners for interrogation; wiretap telephone lines, recording conversations with cassette recorders; rescue downed aircrews and Free World prisoners of war; recover sensitive items in enemy territory; emplace harassing mines and booby traps on infiltration trails and in base areas; conduct certain psychological operations; and perform counterintelligence and deception measures. Base areas and infiltration routes in the border regions were their main focus. These operations were conducted by small USSF and indigenous reconnaissance teams and roadrunner teams posing as VC. The battalion-size reaction forces assigned to the projects had the primary mission of aiding in their extraction if compromised and engaged, but also conducted economy-of-force operations.

Doctrine and training

MIKE Force doctrine

MIKE Force doctrine and tactics were based on US Army light infantry and counterinsurgency tactics and techniques, with significant modifications demanded by the terrain and enemy as well as the imagination of USSF soldiers, who felt unconstrained by conventional tactics. Missions entailed camp reinforcement, camp relief, reconnaissance-in-force, recovery missions, raids, and independent offensive operations along with airborne and airmobile operations.

Units seldom operated as an entity. Platoons, companies, and battalions could be detached for independent missions. Different units could conduct search and clear operations in one area: a couple of companies might be securing CIDG camps under construction, another company might be undergoing refresher training, and yet another detailed to secure the base camp.

The missions assigned MIKE Forces varied from corps to corps. The I Corps MIKE Force was mainly used for reinforcing camps. The others did this too, but the II and III Corps MIKE Forces mostly conducted reconnaissance-in-force operations for their respective field forces and some independent missions. The 2d tended to conduct battalion-size operations and the 3d usually operated as a brigade-size force rotating battalions with two in the

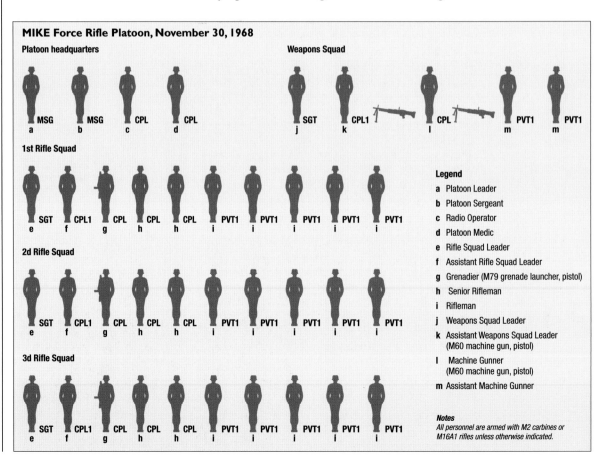

MIKE Force Rifle Platoon, November 30, 1968

Platoon headquarters

MSG a · MSG b · CPL c · CPL d

Weapons Squad

SGT j · CPL1 k · CPL l · PVT1 m · PVT1 m

1st Rifle Squad

SGT e · CPL1 f · CPL g · CPL h · CPL h · PVT1 i · PVT1 i · PVT1 i · PVT1 i · PVT1 i

2d Rifle Squad

SGT e · CPL1 f · CPL g · CPL h · CPL h · PVT1 i · PVT1 i · PVT1 i · PVT1 i · PVT1 i

3d Rifle Squad

SGT e · CPL1 f · CPL g · CPL h · CPL h · PVT1 i · PVT1 i · PVT1 i · PVT1 i · PVT1 i

Legend

a Platoon Leader
b Platoon Sergeant
c Radio Operator
d Platoon Medic
e Rifle Squad Leader
f Assistant Rifle Squad Leader
g Grenadier (M79 grenade launcher, pistol)
h Senior Rifleman
i Rifleman
j Weapons Squad Leader
k Assistant Weapons Squad Leader (M60 machine gun, pistol)
l Machine Gunner (M60 machine gun, pistol)
m Assistant Machine Gunner

Notes
All personnel are armed with M2 carbines or M16A1 rifles unless otherwise indicated.

field. The IV Corps MIKE Force conducted its own independent missions while the Nha Trang MIKE Force conducted brigade-size operations in conjunction with CSFs in any CTZ.

The primary mission, camp relief and reinforcement, could be accomplished by several means. One or more companies could be delivered to the camp, usually by helicopter or air transports; most camps possessed an airstrip. Some (such as those in the mountainous I CTZ and the inundated Mekong Delta IV CTZ) lacked airstrips, but had helicopter landing zones. Camps were relatively small and could only hold one or two MIKE Force companies beyond their own three or four companies. In some cases an MSF company dug in, wired, and emplaced Claymore mines in a position immediately outside the camp's wire, especially on the side it was most likely to be attacked from. MSF companies would also occupy hills and ridges overlooking the endangered camp, especially those within 1,000m. This denied to the enemy the terrain on which to position machine guns, recoilless rifles, and mortars, which could be used to support his attack. Search-and-destroy sweeps and reconnaissance-in-force operations would be conducted up to several kilometers around the camp. They would establish night ambushes on avenues of approach to the camp. The camps actually preferred for the MIKE Force to operate outside the camp. There tended to be conflicts with the camp strikers (owing to the elitist nature of MIKE Forces) and there may have been ethnic conflicts. The real problems, though, were caused by theft of personal possessions and clandestine liaisons with the camp strikers' wives and daughters. This sometimes resulted in firefights between the two groups, although these seldom got out of hand.

Conventional combat missions, usually in the form of reconnaissance-in-force operations, occupied much of the MIKE Forces' time. These were usually conducted in conjunction with CSFs or US units. They might be of battalion or company size. Often, task forces were formed with combinations of MIKE Force and camp companies. These could be under the control of an MSF battalion or the CSF. Sometimes one or two MSF companies were attached to US battalions or brigades for short-term operations. Battalions usually established a forward operating base (FOB) or mission support site (MSS) from which it operated, usually a Strike Force camp. This would serve as the rear base for logistics, communications, and coordinating fire and air support. A reaction force might be on standby there, often provided by the CSF.

The mission of securing sites where camps were under construction was important. Strike camps were built in remote areas generally under VC control and situated on infiltration routes leading out of Laos and Cambodia or in areas where the VC were making major efforts to control the population and resources (food supplies). The VC/NVA knew that the most opportune time to prevent the establishment of a camp was when it was under construction and before the CSF was recruited and trained. MIKE Force companies would secure the camp site for the Army engineer or Navy Seabee builders, secure key terrain near the camp, conduct aggressive combat patrols and ambushes throughout the area, secure local villages to protect the population from VC propaganda and intimidation, provide medical assistance to win the villagers over to the government, and protect recruiters.

Recovery missions were usually platoon or company-size quick-response operations. The MSF would be inserted by helicopter to recover the remains of aircrew from downed aircraft, the remains of ground troops left behind in earlier engagements, downed reconnaissance drone aircraft, or separated troops.

Two members of the II CTZ MIKE Force in "tigers" on a practice firing range. The green beret was not worn during combat operations. (David Lucier)

The American USSF and Australian AATTV members of Detachment A-218 of 3d Battalion, II CTZ MIKE Force after the 1969 "Happy Valley" operation. (Stan Wheeler)

A 5th MSF USSF medic and the nine indigenous medics he trained at their Nha Trang base. The name tapes over their left breast pockets say MIKE FORCE in black over olive drab. Most wear US jumpwings on the tape. (Scott Whitting)

LLDB and MIKE Force strikers arrive at Camp Kham Duc (A-105) in I CTZ, where training was provided to MIKE Force, CSF, and MACV-SOG personnel. (Virgil R. Carter)

Parachute training for the I CTZ MIKE Force at Da Nang. This was usually presented in a two-week course with two or three jumps made. The strikers were awarded US jumpwings rather than Vietnamese ones. (Eugene Makowski)

An Australian warrant officer presents training in small-unit movement formations to an M2 carbine-armed Koho Montagnard company, I CTZ MIKE Force outside of Da Nang. They wear olive drab ARVN field caps with the tiger-stripes. (Virgil R. Carter)

USSF NCOs of the I CTZ MIKE Force coach strikers on the use of the .30-cal. M1918A2 Browning automatic rifle. In the base camp USSF wore standard olive green jungle fatigues rather than tiger-stripes. (Virgil R. Carter)

MIKE Force logistical support was provided through the 5th SFGA's Logistics Support Center at Nha Trang. General supplies, rations, ammunition, replacement weapons, fuel, and everything else needed by MIKE Forces were distributed from the Logisitical Support Center (LSC) to the C-team supporting the MSF.

Eagle Flight tactics

The platoon-size Eagle Flights had little reinforcing capability for camps in danger, but they could support CSF companies conducting operations in the area of operations. They proved to be especially useful in locating scattered USSF and strikers who may have become separated from their units. Normally five Hueys were used for the troop lift, one to extract any prisoners, and four or five gunships for fire support.

They were also used to conduct aerial search sweeps looking for VC activity. When a small enemy element was detected the four squads would be inserted at different points to box in the enemy and attack them from different directions or prevent them from escaping. They were especially useful in pursuit operations when VC who attacked a camp were withdrawing in small groups. Withdrawing enemy would be detected and squads inserted in blocking positions. The command element would remain aloft in the command and control helicopter when the squads were inserted to detect enemy movement, direct the squads, coordinate and direct gunship and artillery fire, and scout beyond the area in which the squads were operating to detect enemy reaction forces moving toward the insertion. Airborne rescue teams of USSF personnel also supported Eagle Flight operations by recovering dead and wounded from downed helicopters as well as weapons, radios, sensitive documents and materials, and destroying the aircraft with demolitions. They also flew night missions using new night vision devices to detect and engage VC units moving under the cover of darkness.

MIKE Force tactics

MIKE Force tactics tended to be straightforward and uncomplicated. Complex plans were avoided owing to the level of training and experience of the strikers and the less than robust command and control system, limited by numbers and range of radios.

Movement formations were simple. In densely vegetated or broken terrain, especially in the hills and mountains, companies often moved in the "long green line," a simple single-file column. Dense vegetation – be it underbrush, bamboo, closely spaced trees and saplings, or high elephant grass – made this essential. Conventional wisdom said that units should deploy in extended formations regardless of the vegetation, and deploy flank security. This was entirely impractical. If moving in extended skirmish lines or wedge formations, each man had to break his own path. This was exhausting, made far too much noise, left easier to follow trails, prevented men from adequately observing threats, and most importantly, was extremely slow. Individual movement rates were uneven and with visibility reduced to a few meters or less made it impossible to maintain formation and direction. Men lagged behind and even became separated. Flank security was seldom employed under such condition, as they were forced to travel slower than the main column because they had to break down brush, and if out of visual contact with the column they could be easily mistaken for the enemy. In open terrain, units would move in extended skirmish or wedge formations.

When contact was imminent companies would assume skirmish-line formations. They could have all three platoons on line; two platoons on line and one to the rear, which might still move in a column so it could move to either flank or protect the rear; or even one platoon forward and two to the rear to extend to either flank, either coming on line or maneuvering to outflank the enemy. A box formation was sometimes used.

The USSF personnel were to be separated within a company formation so that if one became a casualty the others would not be hit. They were also not to be too close to the point of the formation so that they would not be pinned down in the initial engagement. This allowed them to maneuver the rest of the company to the flanks and call for and adjust artillery or air strikes. In theory, when LLDB were present, the USSF personnel were to allow the LLDB to be in a more forward position so that it appeared they were in change. This was an important consideration with regards to their saving

MIKE Force company movement formations

Each line represents a platoon. The triangle indicates the command group.

A Three platoons on line – skirmish line.

B Two platoons on line forward, one to the rear in support.

C Two platoons on line forward, one in column to the rear.

D One platoon on line forward, and two on line following to the rear.

E Box formation.

face. It was not always adhered to, though, as the Americans tended to control the operation.

Machine guns were normally attached to platoons rather than operating as a section under company control. More machine guns were often available than specified by the TOE. They were positioned well forward where they could cover as much of the platoon's zone as possible. They would not be placed in the point, though, in order to prevent them from being hit in the first barrage of fire or pinned down and separated from the platoon. Grenadiers with M79 grenade launchers were positioned near the squad's center when on line.

Movement at night was seldom undertaken because of the danger of ambush. A moving unit made a great deal of noise and was extremely slow unless on a trail or road, in which case ambush was invited. If moving at night cross-country the noise alerted an enemy force, which could easily withdraw or quietly move into an ambush position. Companies usually coiled up at night in a "remain over night" (RON) position, either in a triangle or irregular circle.

Helicopters were essential to infantry operations in Vietnam. They provided troop airlift and insertion into the AO, aerial surveillance and reconnaissance, resupply, medical evacuation (medevac), command and control, fire support, and extraction. Airmobile operations became routine for every infantry unit. They were used not only to insert a unit, but also to

5th MSF troops practice re-righting an RB-15 pneumatic boat off the beach from their Nha Trang base camp. The USSF NCO in the foreground provides guidance.

rapidly reposition it to another area where enemy activity was detected. MSF reconnaissance elements relied heavily on helicopters for a constant series of insertions, extractions, and reinsertions to allow them to cover wide areas. The MSF companies would then respond to detected enemy activity and be inserted to deal with it. This might be a company extracted from elsewhere in the field or one on alert at an airstrip.

US Army and Marine attack helicopter support was provided along with Air Force forward air controllers and close air support, including fixed-wing gunships. Army, Marine, and ARVN field artillery units provided fire support. The IV CTZ MIKE Force conducted occasional small-scale amphibious operations using US Navy landing craft and other small craft. MIKE Forces frequently conducted combined operations with US Army and Marines, ARVN, CSFs, Vietnamese Ranger battalions and Regional Forces, and National Police. CSF companies frequently worked with MSF units operating in their TAOR, if not directly with them, as blocking forces and reserves.

Often one MSF company remained on 24-hour alert in the base to reinforce committed companies or support an endangered camp. It could be helicoptered to the needed area. Companies remaining at the base also provided security.

Trucks were used to move MSF companies from their base camps to departure airfields where they were picked up by helicopters or transports. Two-engine C-123 Providers and four-engine C-130 Hercules transports were often used to deploy MIKE Forces to a CIDG camp's airstrip or another airstrip under Free World control. From there they might be helicoptered, trucked, or marched into their AO.

MSF reconnaissance platoons and companies relied heavily on helicopter insertion and extraction. The concept was for reconnaissance squads (teams) and platoons to be inserted in areas adjacent to where MSF companies and battalions were operating and search for signs of enemy activity. If they made

Recondo School students practice calling for and directing artillery fire on Hon Tri Island off the coast from Nha Trang. They also learned to direct close air support strikes.

contact they could withdraw. There were often other reconnaissance platoons or MSF platoons/companies on standby to reinforce engaged reconnaissance elements. They were often up-gunned in order to fight their way out of engagements with superior forces. In some reconnaissance platoons every squad was provided with a machine gun. They also had priority for M16A1 rifles. If unobserved while detecting enemy activity, they would report to the MSFC and guide in reaction forces or call for and direct artillery and air strikes. If an area proved to be a "dry hole" then they would be extracted and re-inserted by helicopter in other areas or move there by foot. When helicopters were not available they were restricted to conducting short-range foot patrols, greatly reducing their effectiveness. They were also used for combat patrols, small-scale raids, and ambushes. Prior to the implementation of the brigade-size MSFCs with reconnaissance companies, a reconnaissance platoon was often paired up with an MSF company.

Upon returning to base from an operation, companies cleaned weapons and equipment and were usually given three to five days' leave to spend time with their families. Upon return they would spend two or three days preparing for the next operation or would absorb recruits and conduct refresher training for up to three weeks.

A reconnaissance team practices a tight movement formation on open ground, before practising in dense vegetation. In reality, if on open ground they would be much more dispersed.

Mobile Guerrilla Force tactics

Mobile Guerrilla Force missions were codenamed BLACKJACK followed by a two-digit number, the first identifying the CTZ. They were to be inserted covertly into the AO, ether by helicopter (usually done in one lift rather than multiples, with deception landings in other areas) or by covert overland movement, the most common and preferred method. Sometimes the reconnaissance platoon would be inserted first to check the immediate area, establish an initial patrol base, and receive a supply drop before the rest of the MGF arrived. The MGF operated as guerrillas conducting hit-and-run attacks, raids, ambushes, destroying supply caches, and carrying out harassing actions (sniping, mining trails, booby-trapping). They had complete freedom of action. They established temporary patrol bases and sent out reconnaissance teams to locate enemy activity, trails, water points, and camps. Platoons would then move out to take action. The USSF would also conduct an assessment of the area to determine its suitability for future operations. Resupply of ammunition, rations, and uniforms (which wore out quickly) was usually conducted by dropping them in empty napalm bomb containers from Air Commando A-1E Skyraider prop fighter-bombers rather than by helicopter or parachute, which would have attracted too much attention. The Skyraiders appeared only to be making harassing attack runs. This means was not foolproof as once the MGF's presence was detected its location could be determined by the resupply drops.

Many tactics and techniques were employed by MGFs. An example is the stay-behind ambush established by the "tail gunner." When an MGF company was on the move a reconnaissance section securing the column's rear would periodically establish an ambush on the back-trail for 15–30 minutes. It would

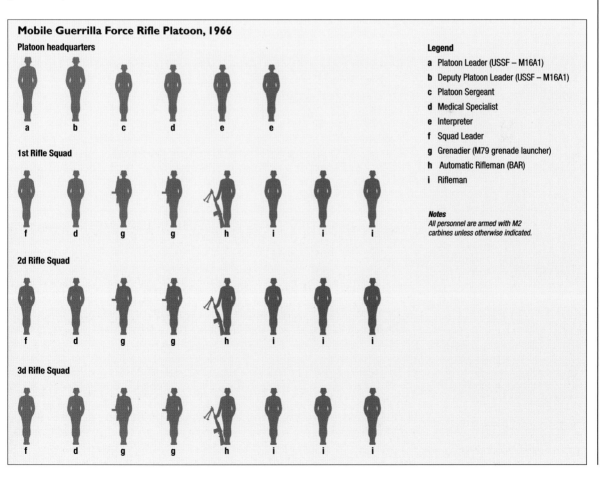

Mobile Guerrilla Force Rifle Platoon, 1966

Platoon headquarters

a   b   c   d   e   e

1st Rifle Squad

f   d   g   g   h   i   i   i

2d Rifle Squad

f   d   g   g   h   i   i   i

3d Rifle Squad

f   d   g   g   h   i   i   i

Legend

a Platoon Leader (USSF – M16A1)
b Deputy Platoon Leader (USSF – M16A1)
c Platoon Sergeant
d Medical Specialist
e Interpreter
f Squad Leader
g Grenadier (M79 grenade launcher)
h Automatic Rifleman (BAR)
i Rifleman

Notes
All personnel are armed with M2 carbines unless otherwise indicated.

move on if no enemy trackers were encountered. It might leave anti-personnel mines or booby traps on the trail.

The guerrilla warfare operational areas were out of artillery range and the MGFs relied on close air support for fire support, which required a delay before it arrived. While they attempted to operate as guerrillas, it was not completely feasible. They could not live off the land as they were on the move, had no support from the civilian population, could not blend into the population, did not know the terrain as local guerrillas would, relied on aerial resupply (which was detectable and at the mercy of the weather), relied on temperamental long-range radio communications, and had no safe haven to flee to. Medical evacuation of sick and wounded was a serious problem and hampered the unit's movements if carried with them. Once its presence was detected, the VC could marshal forces and attempt to pursue the MGF to destroy it or drive it from the area.

It is often said that the MGFs and MSFs were much the same, but in reality they operated differently. The MSFs were reaction and reinforcement units conducting conventional operations while the MGFs attempted to operate as covert guerrillas. The long-duration BLACKJACK operations were found impractical, even though they did inflict damage on the enemy. The MGFs were absorbed into the MIKE Forces as MSF companies in early 1967. They still sometimes conducted BLACKJACK operations, but of much shorter duration.

One example of how MGFs operated was Operation WARBONNET, conducted in I CTZ with the Marines and initiated through Project DELTA contacts. Two 1st MSF companies were committed for MGF operations. To maintain the operational tempo and troop morale, and to reduce combat fatigue the companies were rotated. This proved to be effective since the operation lasted from December 26, 1967 to February 11, 1968 and was a reason cited for very light striker casualties.

Special reconnaissance tactics

The reconnaissance projects typically focused on a specific area rather than conducting missions spread over a wide area. This might be a base area, which could cover up to a couple of hundred square kilometers, or a remote area through which infiltration trails ran. An FOB/MSS would be established at a CIDG camp or some other nearby Free World base. A detailed area assessment would be conducted and all available intelligence on enemy activity collected. The reconnaissance teams (RTs) were given areas to operate in and precise mission objectives. Landing zones were selected along with a general route. RTs deviated from planned routes according to the terrain, vegetation, and enemy activity. Tentative pick-up zones were selected. Communications plans were developed. This was essential as reconnaissance team AOs were usually out of radio range of the FOB/MSS. This usually required radio relay aircraft, which would orbit over the AO at specified times. An AO was a six-kilometer-square "box" and no aircraft could deliver ordnance into it without permission of the RT leader. RT AOs were usually designated by phonetic letters – Alpha, Bravo, Charlie. The RTs planned their missions and presented detailed briefbacks on all aspects to the planning staff. Mission planning and preparations might last up to seven days. Weapons and radios were tested and reaction force plans made. This force might be needed to aid in the extraction of a compromised RT or to exploit a target of opportunity discovered by an RT. It was the exploitation forces that usually conducted BDA missions, although RTs also performed BDA sometimes, being inserted immediately after B-52 bomber Ace Light strikes.

RTs were inserted by helicopters in complex operations requiring several aircraft – typically one command and control bird, an insertion chopper for the RT, two recovery birds for backup and rescue, and two escorting gunships. Multiple landing zones (LZs) were selected and false insertions were made in

---

the area before and after the team was actually inserted, to mislead the enemy. Another technique was for a formation of three helicopters to fly low in trail formation and slightly separated. One chopper would land and off-load an RT and rejoin the others. The multiple helicopter sounds made it difficult to determine if one had set down for a few seconds. LZs were scarce in the rugged terrain and the VC either emplaced anti-helicopter obstacles, hid punji stakes in the high grass, or placed lookouts to warn their own reaction forces. There were instances when RTs were inserted and compromised within minutes. They were often extracted and reinserted elsewhere in their AO. Another method was to insert a reaction force company accompanied by an RT for a raid. The company would be extracted and the RT would remain – a stay-behind insertion. Besides landing on the ground, RTs could repel in using ropes if suitable LZs were unavailable. RTs were usually inserted just before last light to allow the LZs to be located and provide time for the RT to move well away and hideout over the night, which would make tracking very difficult.

RTs moved very slowly and cautiously, sometimes only a few hundred meters a day. They coiled up for the night in areas of dense vegetation in a RON position. They might make communication two or three times a day, reporting their progress and

intelligence information. A communications aircraft usually remained aloft over the AO during daylight hours to react to calls for extraction or air support. RTs sometimes wore black or green uniforms and appropriate headgear to look like VC from a distance.

Extreme caution was used when reconnoitering objectives. An RT might be directed to approach a suspected enemy base camp and place it under surveillance to determine if it was being utilized, and if so the extent and what type of activities were being conducted. If surveillance detected no activity the team would move in closer to the camp to determine if it was occupied. If it appeared to be abandoned they would carefully search it to determine how long it had been vacant, what type of activity had taken place, and if it appeared to be left in a condition indicating it might be reoccupied in the future. For example, had it been used to quarter troops, as a training site, a way-station, or supply transfer point? Trail, road, or canal watch was another important and frequent mission. The infiltration trails were networks and it had to be learned which trails were being used, the extent of traffic, and what was coming down the trail. The NVA frequently swept the trails as much as a

Reconnaissance teams sometimes used the STABO harness for extraction named after the inventors in 1968: MAJ Robert L. Stevens, CPT John D. H. Knabb, and SFC Clifford L. Roberts of the Recondo School. The harness was incorporated in web gear. The UH-1H extraction helicopter dropped a 120ft. rope for each man, the rolled-up leg straps were fastened, and the rope's snaphook fastened to the harness. A disadvantage was that roadrunner teams could not use it, as they had to wear VC equipment.

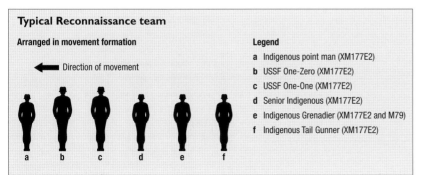

Typical Reconnaissance team

Arranged in movement formation

← Direction of movement

Legend
a Indigenous point man (XM177E2)
b USSF One-Zero (XM177E2)
c USSF One-One (XM177E2)
d Senior Indigenous (XM177E2)
e Indigenous Grenadier (XM177E2 and M79)
f Indigenous Tail Gunner (XM177E2)

a   b   c   d   e   f

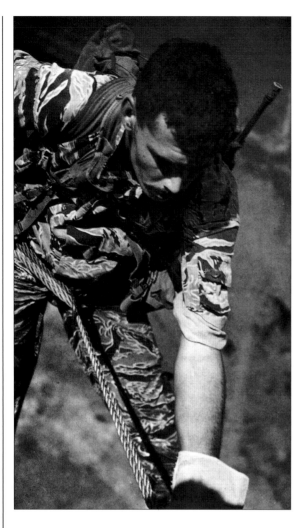

Repelling from a helicopter allowed reconnaissance teams to be inserted into brush-covered landing zones. Two double 120ft. nylon ropes were rigged on either side of the helicopter, allowing four men to repel in at once from about 50ft.

kilometer on either side; more often than not RTs were unable to get close to the trails. Multiple reports on different sectors of the trails over a period of time helped determine what future enemy actions might occur. RTs were often inserted in AOs in which no enemy activity was found. This was valuable because it was important to know where the enemy was not.

The early operations, especially those conducted by Project DELTA, were sometimes costly as techniques of operation were learned through trial and error. The areas these RTs operated in were filled with enemy troops and installations. If it was determined RTs were operating in an area, the VC sent all available troops to conduct sweeps, even inexperienced service troops – anything to flush out the RTs. As the RTs became more effective and difficult to detect, the NVA formed special anti-reconnaissance units to search for and track them.

Roadrunner teams comprised specially trained Vietnamese, who were uniformed, equipped, armed, and carrying the necessary documents to enable them to pose as VC. They did not attempt to intermingle with VC, but would reconnoiter trails and report the locations of base camps, way-stations, caches and the like. If they were seen they might be ignored or if questioned they could often convince real VC they were friends. A roadrunner team would establish a patrol base some distance from the trail and report back there after exploring a trail to transmit intelligence information. More usually, they simply reported information after they were extracted.

Pre-planned extraction points were selected, but if detected or compromised they would call for immediate extraction. Even if they broke contact, extraction was necessary as the enemy now knew of their presence. Extractions were conducted with the command and control chopper arriving first to locate and identify the team's marker panel in a prearranged pattern and make radio contact. If a suitable pick-up zone (PZ) was unavailable then RTs might be extracted by McGuire extraction rigs and STABO extraction harnesses ("strings," as they were known) or 80ft. wire ladders with steel rungs.

The projects' reaction forces aided RTs in trouble, assisted with extractions, and responded to intelligence finds. For example, RTs might discover ammunition, weapons, and supply caches guarded by few or no enemy troops. A reaction force could be quickly inserted to remove or destroy the cache. The RT would be extracted with them, as their mission was now compromised.

Individual and unit training

Individual striker training varied. While CIDG training centers existed, often MIKE Forces simply provided basic training to their recruits themselves, usually six weeks' worth, which was adequate for only the most basic skills. This was increased to eight weeks in 1968. The rest was learned in frequent refresher courses and on-the-job training. Some recruits had previously served in CSFs, other MIKE Forces, and paramilitary forces. Their experience was valuable and some may have been given leadership positions.

Training courses varied in content and were dependent upon available time and resources. There was no standard course other than guidelines provided by 5th SFGA.

Six-week recruit training program, II CTZ MSF, 1968		
Subject	**Hours (day/night)**	**Content**
Processing	16	Issue equipment, identification, billeting, medical clearance, marching in and out of camp procedure.
Commander's time	12	Training directed by supervisor, reinforcement training.
Care and cleaning	10	Weapons and equipment maintenance.
Personal hygiene	4	Preventive measures, basic first-aid.
Physical training	30	PT, obstacle course, sports (soccer, volleyball).
Weapons handling	36	Training on all company weapons, range firing.
Patrolling	20	Squad, platoon, and company patrolling.
Battle drills	12	Fire and maneuver techniques.
Immediate actions	12	Concept and principles of immediate action drills.
Ambush training	6 / 6	Day and night ambush and counter-ambush techniques.
VC tactics	4	VC raids and ambush techniques.
Search and destroy	12	Planning and conduct of search and cordon operations.
River crossing	12	Flotation techniques, tactical and non-tactical crossings.
Demolitions	4	Claymore mines, trip and hand flares.
Night jungle base	8	Occupying a night base, clearing patrols.
Field training exercise	5 days	Deployment to AO, practice of techniques covered in training.

Training was constantly hampered by shortages of USSF/AATTV personnel, qualified striker leaders, constant operational commitments, desertions, inadequate training facilities and equipment, and limited time.

When units were established they typically undertook two to three months' initial training to prepare them for operations, though it was often less. Closely observed by USSF advisors providing the training, leaders were selected at all echelons. They often lacked any formal leadership training, but were selected as having demonstrated natural leadership qualities, a sense of responsibility, maturity, and an aptitude to work with the advisors. There were instances, though, when leaders were elected; this seldom worked. The unit training covered light infantry tactics and weapons employment, comprising only basic combat skills. Such courses culminated in a week-long graduation exercise in the form of a combat patrol in a semi-secure area, but contact with the enemy was possible.

Specialty training courses were conducted as necessary, as was refresher training for units and individuals. For example, crew-served weapons teams, medics, leaders, and platoons and companies, would undertake two- to four-week courses. A unit four-week refresher course might include squad and platoon tactics, weapons proficiency, hand-to-hand combat, and physical fitness. Such training was given to units between operations and was actually a rest period. It was common for several companies to be conducting operations and others undertaking refresher training while a newly raised company underwent initial training.

The MSF Training Center was established in mid-1968 at An Khe, II CTZ under the LLDB with USSF advisors. The short-lived operation was closed on October 23, 1969. It provided refresher training for countrywide MSF battalions in a three-week course, as well as basic individual training with some 75 percent of the training in the field. Some MIKE Force strikers were trained at the CIDG Training Center at Trang Sup, III CTZ under A-301. This was mainly for training CSF troops.

Parachute school lasted six or seven days. The course conducted by II CTZ MSF in 1968 included four days of ground training, with a jump without equipment on the fifth and an equipment jump on the sixth. Other courses sometimes provided three jumps; by comparison, the three-week Ft Benning Parachute Course required five jumps. With the high turnover rate it was difficult for any given company to maintain jump status. Only a few companies were parachute qualified at any one time. Jump training was conducted by the MIKE Forces themselves or in a formal two-week course at the LLDB Training Center at Dong Ba Thin run by B-51. This school could train one 132-man MSF company per month in a three-week course, but if necessary increased-tempo training could qualify one battalion a month. It also provided a five-week CRP course.

Difficulties were occasionally encountered with the quality of personnel. An early 1966 report on the I Corps MIKE Force revealed the following:

> It has become evident that the MIKE Force is not ready to conduct company-size operations; the CIDG platoon leaders have no eye for the ground and are reluctant to coordinate their platoon movements with that of other platoons and the rest of the company. The soldiers are also unwilling to expose themselves to physical discomforts, fatigue, hunger, etc.

Disciplinary power was necessary to motivate the strikers and improve their performance, and refresher training cycles were increased. Discipline could comprise minor corporal punishment, extra duty, fines, confinement, and dismissal from the Force. USSF NCOs could fire troublesome strikers on the spot by filling out a brief "termination of employment" form. If Vietnamese, they might be turned over to the ARVN for conscription. They fell under no military legal system. If a striker committed a civil crime he fell under the Vietnamese civilian legal system.

The maintenance of MIKE Force morale was a continuing problem. Efforts were made to improve base camp living conditions, increase pay, provide adequate uniforms, and present decorations. The CIDG were authorized the award of the US Commendation Medal and Bronze Star, both with "V" devices for valor, as well as the Vietnamese Gallantry Cross with Bronze Star. Some units wore different-colored scarves for each company and were presented guidon streamers commemorating successful operations. Early shortages of tiger-stripe uniforms and Bata boots[4] in Asian sizes even had adverse morale effects. Strikers considered tiger-stripes a prestige uniform, but many units were forced to issue olive green fatigues and mixed uniforms. Often, worn-out or much repaired "tigers" had to be donned. There was also a tendency during the February Tet holiday for numerous strikers to return home without leave to visit families. Most returned, but some did not and had to be replaced.

Recruiting was an on-going effort and a major complication. Because of casualties, illness, desertions, resignations, dismissal, and release upon completion of contract, MIKE Forces were constantly in need of recruits. There was no central recruiting command; each MIKE Force had to handle its own recruiting. Many troops were recruited from remote villages. Others, except the Montagnards, came from large towns and cities. Being ethnic minorities they were usually exempt from conscription by the ARVN. The Vietnamese government did not consider most minorities, even though born in Vietnam, to be full citizens. These men joined because they needed jobs, and the pay was good by Vietnamese standards; many belonged to groups with political agendas and sought military experience for later use against the Vietnamese, and some sincerely wished to fight the communist enemy or defend their homes.

---

4 "Tigers" were issued to all CIDG strikers and worn by USSF on operations, and became a distinctive symbol. "Batas" were Canadian-made canvas and rubber jungle boots.

Recruiting teams comprising Americans, Australians, and appropriate indigenous personnel were dispatched to cities and towns where personnel of the desired ethnic groups could be recruited. Recruiting teams also visited local villages. Early recruiting efforts were hampered owing to promises made by indigenous recruiters of unreasonably high pay, leadership positions, or low-risk or even "palace guard" conditions. Another problem was that indigenous recruiters tended to recruit for their own platoons or companies. There were also incidents of harassment by LLDB and local ARVN units, creating much tension. All this resulted in misunderstandings, resignations, desertions, and refusals to conduct operations. In such cases the troops were disarmed, equipment confiscated, and they were turned out of the camp. It was learned that formal enlistment contracts specifying pay, position, duties, and period (six or 12 months) were necessary.

One problem experienced was the backdoor recruiting of experienced MIKE Force troops by other organizations – for example, special reconnaissance projects, MACV-SOG Special Commando Unit, Provincial Reconnaissance Unit (PRU), among others. The less intense life of the CSF attracted some strikers after the pace and perils of MSF operations.

Ethnic considerations were critical. A particular MIKE Force might indeed be manned by so-called "Montagnards," for example, but they might be from several tribes (of which there were 16 main groups). They were usually organized into companies according to tribe, although certain tribal groups could serve in the same companies. There were other ethnic groups, including Khmers (Vietnamese-born Cambodians), Nungs (Chinese/Thai), Cham (Malayo-Polynesian), Meo (Mongoloid/Caucasoid), and there were also religious considerations to be taken into account. While Vietnamese served in some CSFs, very few served in the MIKE Forces. Other ethnic groups resented the Vietnamese owing to the latter's prejudice against ethnic minorities, whom they called *Moa* (savages), and because of the fear that Vietnamese units might include VC sympathizers. To improve morale and reduce desertion rates, the strikers' family members were often relocated in a town near the base or even a village outside the base. Wounded and ill CIDG troops were treated at hospitals operated by each C-team. Their families received treatment from highly trained USSF medics.

The reconnaissance projects conducted their own specialized training of both USSF and indigenous personnel. New USSF RT members underwent initial training and orientation and would then be paired with an experienced RT leader to further their skills through on-the-job training. DELTA's B-52 commenced a formalized training program in May 1964 to prepare RT members. In September 1965 members of the 101st Airborne Division's LRP company attended the course. Seeing the benefits of such specialized training, General Westmoreland directed B-52 to establish and operate the MACV Recondo Training School in Nha Trang on September 15, 1966. Besides training Special Forces and US LRP personnel, other Free World reconnaissance troops attended the three-week course. Of the 5,395 troops who began the course, 3,357 completed it. Training included reconnaissance tactics and techniques; immediate action drills; close-combat techniques; long-range communications; survival, escape and evasion; and directing air strikes. The course included a one-week field exercise on Hon Tra Island off the coast near Nha Trang.

All USSF personnel, regardless of previous experience or rank (field grade officers and sergeants major were exempt) undertook a two-week Combat Orientation Course conducted by the Recondo School to acclimatize and prepare themselves for operations in Vietnam. This included a three-day combat patrol on Hon Tra Island.

Unit organization

The original unofficial MIKE Force patch. It was ordered discontinued owing to the skull and crossbones and the misconstrued meaning of "MF."

Two separate organizations need to be studied when examining the MIKE Force structure: US Special Forces, and the MIKE Forces themselves.

The 5th SFGA was organized in a very different way to other SF groups, and was greatly augmented with additional detachments and units. An SF group normally consisted of a headquarters and headquarters company, four operational companies, and a signal company. The company headquarters was a Special Forces Operational Detachment C, or C-team, commanded by a lieutenant colonel. It had an executive officer (XO), S-1 (personnel), S-2 (intelligence), S-3 (operations), and S-4 (supply) officers, a sergeant major, an NCO assistant for each principal staff officer, and five radio operators. There were three SFOD Bs (B-teams) commanded by a major, but in Vietnam they were often commanded by lieutenants colonel. The B-team had the same staff positions as the C-team, but was rounded out by what was essentially an A-team without its two officers. Under each B-team were four SFODAs (A-teams) – the basic SF operational element. A standard A-team consisted of a captain CO, first lieutenant XO, an operations sergeant, intelligence sergeant, two weapons leaders, two engineer and demolition specialists, two communications NCOs, and two medics – all NCOs of various grades.

In Vietnam this standard organization was abandoned. The basic structure was retained, but manning was increased and TOE specified ranks were ignored. More often than not positions were filled by men a grade or two (sometimes three grades lower) than called for. As many as eight A-teams might be subordinate to a B-team, with each operating a CIDG camp.

A B-team assigned to operate a MIKE Force followed the basic B-team organization. There would be one A-team for each battalion authorized to the MIKE Force. The numbers of officers and NCOs assigned varied greatly as did the allocation of specialists. Rather than two NCOs representing each SF specialty, any mix and number could be found. A-teams could just as easily be over strength as under.

In the early single-battalion MIKE Forces with an A-team, the NCO team members for the most part were company and platoon leaders. It varied from team to team, but usually there was a senior NCO leading each company plus an NCO for each platoon. On other occasions there may have only been two NCOs per company, informally called the commander and XO. In some cases there may have been a third NCO, who did not have a particular duty, but assisted with the control of the company. He may have brought up the rear, moved from platoon to platoon, or could take over a particular platoon. The two

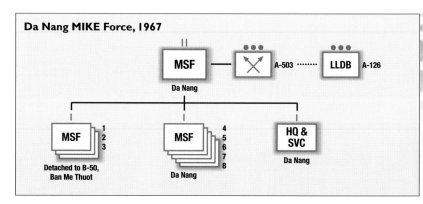

Da Nang MIKE Force, 1967

or three officers assigned to the A-team served as the battalion commander, XO, and either as an operations or logistics officer. The "ops officer" was sometimes described as "one who went on operations," but he may have served as an actual operations or plans officer. One of the officers usually remained in the rear, either at the MIKE Force base or an FOB/MSS from which the MIKE Force was operating. Whether the XO or ops/log officer, his job was to ensure the unit in the field received ammunition, rations, water, supplies, and whatever else was needed. He coordinated medical evacuation and fire support. He would usually be accompanied by a couple of NCOs. They had to monitor the radio 24 hours a day, request ammunition and supplies, request and coordinate helicopters to deliver it, and ensure everything was loaded. They might be assisted by A-team members of the CIDG camp they were operating from.

One example is provided by A-503 in late 1967, which was responsible for the battalion-size 5th MSF. It was assigned four officers and approximately 20 NCOs. The four company commanders were usually master sergeants or sergeants first class assisted by two or three NCOs, one of whom was usually a medic. By the end of the year a fifth rifle company was raised and the A-team's strength slightly increased.

Additionally, two to 12 officers and warrant officers (senior NCOs equivalent to US sergeants major) of the Australian Army Training Team, Vietnam (AATTV, or "The Team") were attached to the A-team and served alongside the USSF as advisors and leaders in the I and II Corps MIKE Forces. There were some AATTV briefly attached to Projects DELTA and OMEGA. It was common for two or three AATTV to provide the leadership for an MSF company along with one or two USSF. These highly experienced and professional soldiers were a valuable asset, though there were occasional difficulties experienced owing to differences in training philosophy and small-unit tactics. Contrary to popular opinion, they were not members of the Australian Special Air Service (ASAS),

An early I CTZ MSF patch, which saw limited use.

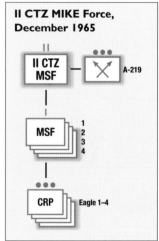

II CTZ MIKE Force, December 1965

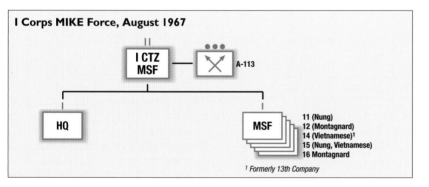

I Corps MIKE Force, August 1967

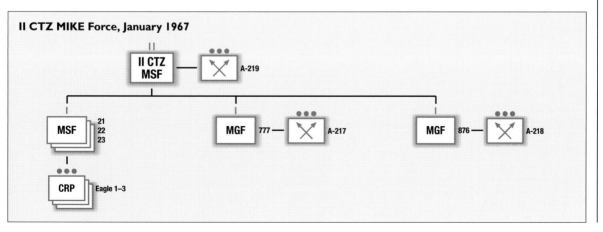

II CTZ MIKE Force, January 1967

although a few had previously served with this formation. Their numbers were reduced and by 1969 few remained assigned to MSFs.

From 1967/68 many MIKE Forces were assigned two or three A-teams without an overseeing B-team. The senior A-team commander was in

Example A-team with USSF and AATTV personnel controlling a MSF battalion	
A-113, I Corps MIKE Force, April 1967	
Detachment CO	Australian captain
Detachment XO	USSF captain
Adjutant	Australian WO1
Quartermaster	Australian WO2
Weapons sergeant	USSF sergeant 1st class
Medical specialist	USSF sergeant
CO, 11th Co	Australian WO2
XO, 11th Co	Australian WO2
Platoon leader, 11th Co	Australian WO2
Platoon leader, 11th Co	Australian WO2
CO, 12th Co	USSF captain
XO, 12th Co	Australian WO2
Platoon leader, 12th Co	USSF sergeant 1st class
CO, 13th Co	Australian WO2
XO, 13th Co	Australian WO2

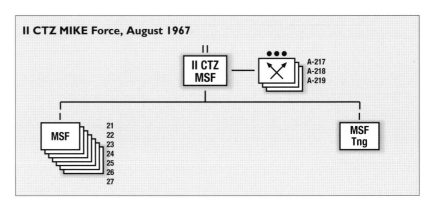

II CTZ MIKE Force, August 1967

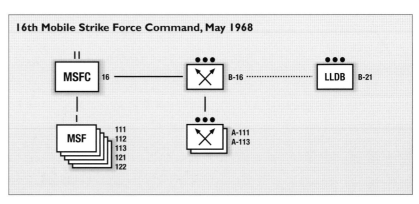

16th Mobile Strike Force Command, May 1968

Mobile Strike Force Commands, 1968/69			
B-16, Co C, 5th SFGA	Da Nang	1st MSFC	A-161, A-162
B-20, Co B, 5th SFGA	Pleiku	2d MSFC	A-204, A-217, A-218, A-219, A-223
B-36, Co A, 5th SFGA	Long Hai	3d MSFC	A-361, A-362, A-363
B-40, Co D, 5th SFGA	Can Tho	4th MSFC	A-401, A-402, A-403, A-404, A-405
B-55, 5th SFGA	Nha Trang	5th MSFC	A-503, A-504
Note that previously the component A-teams may have carried different designations.			

command and the individual A-teams basically lost their identity as their members were assigned to different MSF companies. The USSF identified themselves with the MIKE Force rather than an A-team, the teams becoming merely administrative assignments. In II CTZ in early 1968 each B-team was authorized an MSF company and some grew to a battalion. These were reassigned to the 2d MSFC in 1969.

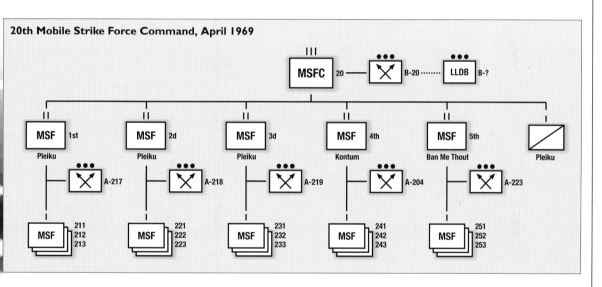

20th Mobile Strike Force Command, April 1969

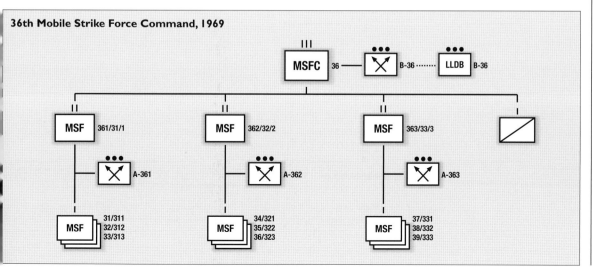

36th Mobile Strike Force Command, 1969

The official October 16, 1968 CIDG Mobile Strike Force sleeve insignia is similar to the Camp Strike Force insignia, but incorporates a black parachute canopy.

A more robust command organization was implemented on May 23, 1968 when the MIKE Forces were enlarged to brigade size and a B-team assigned with multiple A-teams, one per battalion. This established the five Mobile Strike Force Commands (MSFCs).

The 5th MSFC was a countrywide deployable force to back up the corps MIKE Forces. It also conducted its own unilateral operations in any corps area, but mainly in II and III CTZs. These operations were conducted within CSF TAORs. B-55 and its two A-teams were authorized 11 officers and 38 NCOs.

An A-team was authorized for each battalion in the MSFC. The 5th SFGA order directing this reorganization stated:

> Each subject B Detachment is authorized one additional A Detachment for each subordinate MSF battalion for command and control. Each subordinate detachment/battalion will be given three-digit numerical designation in accordance with parent MSFC designation; i.e., Detachment A-161 with the 1st Battalion of 16th MSFC.

In reality, though, the A-teams were not always redesignated to reflect the parent B-team designation. This also resulted in a redesignation of the MSF companies with three-digit numbers. The MIKE Forces experienced difficulties accommodating this expansion because of shortages of USSF personnel (most often medics, radio operators, and weapons specialists), insufficient troop facilities, equipment shortages, and the lack of time and resources to undertake major recruiting efforts. It would require months to implement the expansion.

With an A-team now assigned to each battalion only two or three NCOs provided company leadership and they seldom led platoons. In instances where one or two USSF NCOs were designated as platoon leaders the other platoons would be led by CIDG. Such an A-team might number eight to 14 men. The 3d MSFC in 1969 typically had only seven USSF and six LLDB accompanying each battalion in the field. Each USSF was accompanied by an interpreter if sufficient numbers were available. Most were Vietnamese, while some were Montagnard. In Montagnard units from the more primitive tribes a Vietnamese interpreter might have to have his own "Yard" interpreter to translate into the tribal dialect. Combat interpreters were civilian employees and not strikers, although they were armed and combat trained in the eight-week Combat Interpreter Course at the LLDB Training Center.

It must be pointed out that a team member's specialty had little to do with his actual duties. USSF NCO company commanders, XOs, and platoon leaders could be of any SF specialty. One would think they would be weapons specialists, who were also trained in tactics, but they could just as likely be SF engineers, communications, and medics. An SF medic was just as capable of leading a rifle platoon or company, training his troops in small-unit tactics, and directing air strikes and artillery fire as others. He would also serve as the company medic and could perform minor surgery. He was assisted by indigenous medics, whom he trained. Most SF NCOs had previously served as infantrymen, combat engineers, artillerymen, or in other job skills. This greatly enhanced their flexibility.

Positions were not rock solid either. The positions held by USSF personnel could change between operations. The A-team commander would be the MSF battalion CO, but he could also lead one of the companies and the other officer another, with an NCO leading the third. It all depended on available USSF personnel, the tactical situation, and what worked best for the team.

Regardless of titles as battalion, company, and platoon CO/XO/leader, the USSF personnel were still technically advisors. There were also CIDG striker leaders at company level and below: COs, XOs, first sergeants, and platoon leaders. They ran the companies' day-to-day operations and in combat functioned as a team with their USSF counterparts. This proved to be an

The semi-official sword and lightning bolt MIKE Force patch replaced the skull and crossbones insignia and was mainly used by the 2d and 3d MSF. They remained in use after the official patch was adopted.

40th Mobile Strike Force Command, 1969

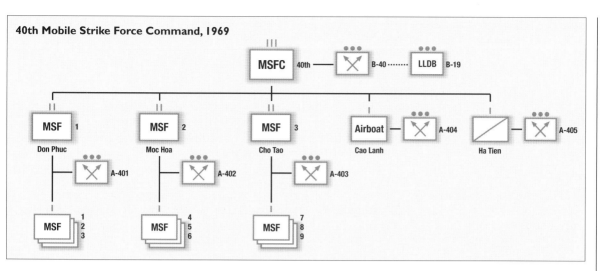

effective method, with the USSF chain-of-command coordinating between elements and making critical decisions while the CIDG leadership implemented action within the unit. The USSF also learned from the experienced striker leadership. It was a cooperative two-way street of command and learning from one another and worked quite well. There were no CIDG leadership positions at battalion or MSFC level.

From 1968 B-teams and multiple A-teams ideally assigned personnel to the following positions, which may have been given different titles in some units.

Example USSF MIKE Force personnel allocation
B-team, MSFC staff
Commanding officer
Executive officer
Adjutant
S-2 (intelligence)
S-3 (operations)
S-4 (supply)
S-5 (civic action/psychological operations)
Sergeant major
Operations sergeant
Intelligence sergeant
Supply sergeant
Communications sergeant
Medical specialist
Administrative supervisor
MSF companies
Commanding officer
Executive officer
Platoon leaders (x 3)
Weapons platoon leader
Company medic

The 5th MSF adopted the semi-official MIKE Force insignia with the addition of a red crossbow owing to it being manned by Montagnards.

The elaborate "dragon patch" was worn only by the USSF of the 2d MSFC, on the left pocket of their jungle uniforms.

Many of the positions would be unfilled, but there might be additional positions assigned to the B-team. A small political warfare team (POLWAR) was usually assigned to support civic action and psychological operations, which were mostly efforts to improve striker morale and assist dependents.

Unit designation practices

As with unit organization there were two systems of unit designation. 5th SFGA C-teams were designated by one-digit numbers as per the CTZ they were responsible for. B-teams carried two-digit numbers beginning with the C-team's number. A-teams had three-digit numbers with the first two being their parent B-team's. B-teams assigned directly to the 5th SFGA were designated in the 50-series as were their A-teams. A-teams directly subordinate to a C-team were identified by the first number being the C-team's, the second a "0", and the third a sequential number; for example, A-301 was assigned directly to C-3. Prior to October 1965 A-teams were deployed on temporary duty from SF groups in the States and on Okinawa, prior to 5th SFGA taking over SF operations in Vietnam in October 1964. Their team numbers did not correspond to the numbering practices used by the 5th SFGA. TDY teams might be designated with any two- or three-digit number.

The MIKE Forces bore more designation variations than any other units, sometimes leading to confusion. The MIKE Forces bore the CTZ number (1st–4th) or the 5th in the case of the 5th SFGA's own. They were also known as the I–IV Corps or CTZ MIKE Forces. In May 1968 the MSFCs were redesignated 16th, 20th, 36th, 40th, and 55th using the designation of their assigned B-teams. They were also called the 1st–4th MSFC relating to the CTZ number plus the 5th MSFC. They were additionally sometimes referred to by their base location, the Nha Trang or the Kontum MIKE Force. The battalions in each MIKE Force were designated by sequential numbers, 1st–5th, with no relationship to the CTZ or B-team number. Originally the companies too were designated in numerical sequence with the single-battalion MIKE Force (1st–5th Companies). In 1967 the companies were given two-digit numbers with the first identifying the corps area (21–29th Companies were in the II Corps MSF). This was implemented at different times by the MSFs. In May/June 1968 they were redesignated with three-digit numbers as CIDG CSF companies with the first number being the CTZ's, or "5" in the 5th MSF, the second digit the parent battalion, and the third the company within the battalion. This meant that the 231st Company was the first company within the 3d Battalion

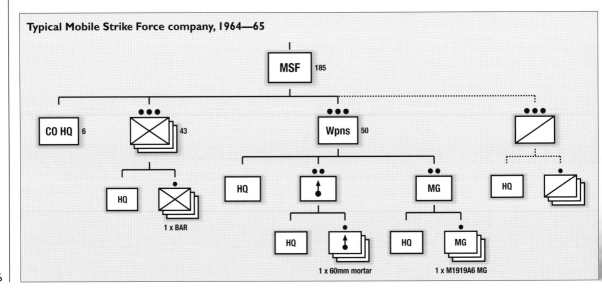

Typical Mobile Strike Force company, 1964—65

of the 2d MSFC. There were changes made in company numbering over the years and it is difficult to track their lineage as some were switched to newly raised battalions and renumbered.

MGFs were assigned three-digit task force numbers, which had no relation to the corps number, C-team, associated A-team, or anything else. They were sometimes assigned other temporary task force designations, such as Task Force Blue.

MIKE Forces were provided tables of organization developed by 5th SFGA. Unit organization was simple and streamlined with a minimum of support elements. The early single battalion MIKE Forces had from three to five companies. The multi-battalion MSFs had three-company battalions. Companies had a small headquarters, three or four three-squad rifle platoons, sometimes with a weapons squad, and a weapons platoon. Some companies had a combat reconnaissance platoon or section. For all practical purposes there were no battalion headquarters companies. There were some minimal service personnel assigned (supply, mechanics, medics, cooks, tailors, barbers) to the battalion, who remained in the base camp. There were either physically disabled CIDG or civilian employees. The battalion headquarters for all practical purposes consisted only of a few USSF, LLDB, and their radio operators and interpreters.

The reconnaissance projects were designated by Greek letters and supposition exists as to their sequence and the existence of other Greek-lettered projects. One myth claims that Project DELTA's original compound was triangular-shaped, as is the Greek letter, but this is untrue. There is no known reason why certain Greek letters were selected. The projects were not organized in any particular sequence and most letters skipped as there was no overall naming scheme. There were no Projects ALPHA or BETA for example, only DELTA, OMEGA, and SIGMA. There was a Project GAMMA (B-57),[5] but it was involved with unilateral deception operations and clandestine intelligence collection and not on-the-ground

---

5 The 52-man B-57 existed from June 1967 and was based in Saigon. It was relocated to Nha Trang in February 1968, designated Project GAMMA in April that year, and inactivated in March 1970.

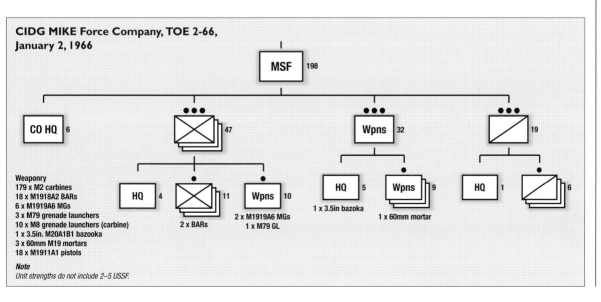

CIDG MIKE Force Company, TOE 2-66, January 2, 1966

MSF 198

CO HQ 6

47

HQ 4
2 x BARs
11
Wpns 10
2 x M1919A6 MGs
1 x M79 GL

Wpns 32
HQ 5
1 x 3.5in bazoka
Wpns 9
1 x 60mm mortar

19
HQ 1
6

Weaponry
179 x M2 carbines
18 x M1918A2 BARs
6 x M1919A6 MGs
3 x M79 grenade launchers
10 x M8 grenade launchers (carbine)
1 x 3.5in. M20A1B1 bazooka
3 x 60mm M19 mortars
18 x M1911A1 pistols

Note
Unit strengths do not include 2–5 USSF.

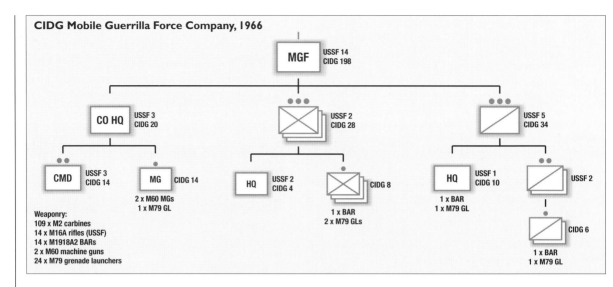

CIDG Mobile Guerrilla Force Company, 1966

MGF — USSF 14 / CIDG 198

CO HQ — USSF 3 / CIDG 20

CMD — USSF 3 / CIDG 14

MG — CIDG 14
2 x M60 MGs
1 x M79 GL

Weaponry:
109 x M2 carbines
14 x M16A rifles (USSF)
14 x M1918A2 BARs
2 x M60 machine guns
24 x M79 grenade launchers

USSF 2 / CIDG 28

HQ — USSF 2 / CIDG 4

CIDG 8
1 x BAR
2 x M79 GLs

USSF 5 / CIDG 34

HQ — USSF 1 / CIDG 10
1 x BAR
1 x M79 GL

USSF 2

CIDG 6
1 x BAR
1 x M79 GL

reconnaissance missions like the other Greek letter projects. While MACV-SOG RTs were named after snakes (CCN), states (CCC), and tools (CCS), the Greek-letter projects' RTs were simply designated Team 1 and so on.

The early MSF companies were organized under locally developed TOEs and varied. A typical company in 1964/65 was organized into a six-man company headquarters, three 43-man rifle platoons with a headquarters, three rifle squads with one BAR, and a 50-man weapons platoon with a headquarters, mortar section, and machine-gun section. The sections had a very small headquarters and two squads, the mortar squads with one 60mm and the machine-gun squads each with two M1919A6 guns. Some companies possessed a small reconnaissance platoon with three, usually six-man, squads.

CIDG MIKE Force Company, TOE 2-66, January 2, 1966		
Company Headquarters	**6 total**	
Company CO	I LT	
Executive officer	I LT	
Company medic	I SGT	
Radio operator	2 CPL	AN/PRC-10
Rifle grenadier	I PFC	carbine w/M8 GL
Rifle Platoon (x3)	**47 total**	
Rifle Platoon HQ	4 total	
Platoon leader	I LT	
Platoon sergeant	I MSG	
Radio operator	I CPL	
Platoon medic	I CPL	
Rifle Squad (x3)	**II total**	
Squad leader	I SGT	
Assistant squad leader	I SGT	carbine w/M8 GL
Automatic rifleman	2 CPL	BAR, .45-cal. pistol
Rifleman	2 CPL	

 (Table continues on page 39)

Rifleman	2 PFC	
Rifleman	3 PVT	
Weapons Squad	**10 total**	
Squad leader	1 SGT	
Gunner, LMG	2 CPL	M1919A6 MG
Assistant gunner	2 CPL	
Ammunition bearer	4 PFC	
Grenadier	1 PFC	M79 GL
Weapons Platoon	**32 total**	
Weapons Platoon HQ	5 total	
Platoon leader	1 LT	
Radio operator	1 CPL	
Platoon medic	1 CPL	
Gunner, 3.5in.	1 PFC	3.5in. bazooka
Assistant gunner	1 PVT	
Weapons Squad (x3)	**9 total**	
Squad leader (gunner)	1 SGT	60mm mortar, carbine
Assistant gunner	1 SGT	
Ammunition preparer	1 CPL	
Ammunition bearer	6 PVT	
Reconnaissance Platoon	**19 total**	
Reconnaissance Platoon HQ	1 total	
Platoon leader	1 LT	
Reconnaissance Squad (x3)	**6 total**	
Squad leader	1 SGT	
Chief scout	1 SGT	
Scout	3 CPL	
Rifleman	1 PFC	
Total strength:	**198 CIDG**	

Notes
All personnel armed with M2 carbines unless indicated otherwise.
2–5 USSF would accompany a company.
One HT-1 radio per company HQ and the five platoon HQs.

On September 1, 1966 the companies were reduced in strength to 156 with the elimination of the CRP and weapons platoon (the company retained one 60mm). To replace the mortars an M79 grenade launcher was assigned to each rifle squad. CRPs were sometimes paired with companies and in other cases consolidated into reconnaissance companies.

The short-lived Mobile Guerrilla Forces consisted of a specially raised USSF A-team, a 150-man strike company, and a 34-man CRP (later to total 198). The company was organized similarly to an MSF company, but lacked the weapons platoon. Instead it had a machine-gun squad as part of the company headquarters – the only heavy weapons (there were no mortars). USSF held the primary leadership positions with three in the headquarters, two in each rifle platoon and three in the reconnaissance platoon. No LLDB were assigned. When absorbed into the MIKE Forces they adopted the standard MSF TOE.

CIDG Mobile Guerrilla Force Company, 1966	
Company Headquarters	**3 USSF, 20 CIDG, 23 total**
Command Section	3 USSF, 14 CIDG, 17 total
Force CO	USSF
Force intelligence specialist	USSF
Force communications specialist	USSF
Force sergeant major	
Force communications specialist (x2)	AN/PRC-74
Radio technician operator	AN/PRC-25
Force medical specialist	
Messengers (x8; 2 detailed per platoon)	
Chief interpreter	
Machine-Gun Squad	**6 CIDG total**
Machine gunner (x2)	M60 MG
Assistant machine gunner (x2)	
Grenadier	M79 GL
Radio technician operator	
Rifle Platoon (x3)	**2 USSF, 28 CIDG, 30 total**
Rifle Platoon HQ	2 USSF, 4 CIDG, 6 total
Platoon leader	USSF
Deputy platoon leader	USSF
Platoon sergeant	
Platoon medical specialist	
Interpreter (x2)	
Rifle Squad (x3)	**8 CIDG total**
Squad leader	
Medical specialist	
Grenadier (x2)	M79 GL
Automatic rifleman	BAR
Rifleman (x3)	
Reconnaissance Platoon	**5 USSF, 34 CIDG, 39 total**
Reconnaissance Platoon HQ	1 USSF, 10 CIDG, 11 total
Force XO/Platoon leader	USSF
Platoon sergeant	
Platoon medical specialist	
Radio technician operator	
Interpreter (x2)	
Fire team leader	
Grenadier	M79 GL
Automatic rifleman	BAR
Rifleman	
Medical specialist	
Reconnaissance Section (x2)	**2 USSF, 12 CIDG, 14 total**

 (Table continues on page 41)

Communications or intelligence specialist	USSF	
Demolition or medical specialist	USSF	
Reconnaissance Squad (x4; two squads per section)	**6 CIDG total**	
Squad leader		
Radio technician operator		
Grenadier		M79 GL
Automatic rifleman		BAR
Rifleman		
Medical specialist		
Total strength:	**14 USSF, 198 CIDG = 212 total**	

Notes
All CIDG personnel armed with M2 carbines unless indicated otherwise. All USSF armed with M16A1 rifles.
HT-1 radios carried by CIDG radio technician operators and most USSF.

From 1968 the multiple-battalion MSFCs consisted of a 227-man headquarters and service company, a 135-man reconnaissance company, and two to five 552-man battalions. In practice these figures varied greatly and units usually fielded fewer strikers. Internal organization varied as well.

In 1968 the MSF company was organized into four rifle platoons rather than the long-established three. It also included a small reconnaissance section (or "platoon") and a mortar "section" (actually a squad) with a single 60mm mortar. Firepower was comparable to that of a US rifle company in Vietnam, which had only three rifle platoons and was often more understrength (US rifle companies had a weapons platoon with three 81mm mortars and two 106mm recoilless rifles, but these were often dissolved in Vietnam). It was not uncommon, though, for MSF companies to field only three platoons. Several USSF NCOs reported they ignored company TOEs and modified organization and armament as necessary. One 5th MSF company was described as having two each of 60mm mortars and 57mm recoilless rifles in the weapons platoon. Whatever was felt necessary for the mission would be carried, from all four weapons to none. Crews not required to man weapons served as riflemen.

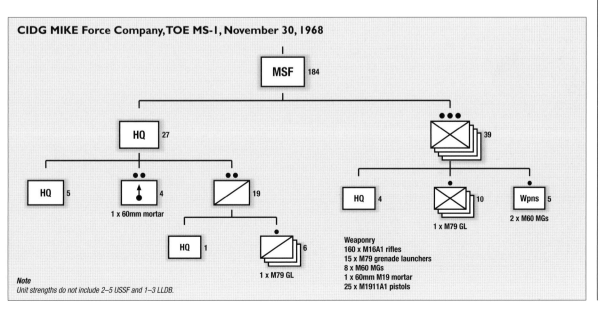

CIDG MIKE Force Company, TOE MS-1, November 30, 1968

Weaponry
160 x M16A1 rifles
15 x M79 grenade launchers
8 x M60 MGs
1 x 60mm M19 mortar
25 x M1911A1 pistols

Note
Unit strengths do not include 2–5 USSF and 1–3 LLDB.

41

CIDG MIKE Force Company, TOE MS-1, November 30, 1968

Company Headquarters	5 total	
Company CO	1 2nd LT	M16A1 rifle, M1911A1 pistol
Executive officer	1 WO	
Company medic	1 WO	
Radio operator	1 SGT	AN/PRC-25
Medic	1 SGT	
Mortar Section	**4 total**	
Section leader	1 MSG	60mm mortar, M1911A1 pistol
Gunner	1 SGT	
Assistant gunner	1 CPL 1	
Ammunition bearer	1 PVT 1	
Reconnaissance Section	**19 total**	
Reconnaissance Section HQ	1 total	
Section leader	1 SGT	
Reconnaissance Squad (x3)	**6 total**	
Squad leader	1 CPL 1	
Scout	2 CPL	
Grenadier	1 CPL	M79 GL, M1911A1 pistol
Rifleman	2 CPL	
Rifle Platoon (x4)	**39 total**	
Rifle Platoon HQ	4 total	
Platoon leader	1 MSG	
Platoon sergeant	1 MSG	
Radio operator	1 CPL	AN/PRC-25
Platoon medic	1 CPL	
Rifle Squad (x3)	**10 total**	
Squad leader	1 SGT	
Assistant squad leader	1 CPL 1	
Grenadier	1 CPL	M79 GL, M1911A1 pistol
Senior rifleman	2 CPL	
Rifleman	5 PVT 1	
Weapons Squad	**5 total**	
Squad leader	1 SGT	
Assistant squad leader	1 CPL 1	M60 MG, M1911A1 pistol
Machine gunner	1 CPL	M60 MG, M1911A1 pistol
Assistant gunner	2 PVT 1	
Total strength:	**184 CIDG**	

Notes

All personnel armed with M16A1 rifles or M2 carbines unless indicated otherwise.

2–5 USSF and 1–3 LLDB would accompany a company.

Two HT-1 radios in the company HQ and the four platoon HQs; one per mortar section, reconnaissance section HQ, and in the three reconnaissance squads.

Eagle Flight organization

An Eagle Flight was a platoon-size unit comprising four ten-man squads as originally developed. Each squad carried a BAR or M1919A6 machine gun. Their organization was based on that of the aerorifle platoon organic to US Army air cavalry troops (one assigned to each armored cavalry squadron of infantry, airborne, mechanized, and armored divisions).

In 1964/65 the two II CTZ Eagle Flight Detachment platoons consisted of a four-man headquarters and two three-squad sections, a squad being six-strikers, a helicopter load (plus room for platoon headquarters and USSF personnel). Up to five USSF advisors accompanied a platoon.

Two five-man USSF rescue teams were part of the program. Each team (Task Forces 1 and 2) consisted of a captain team leader, assistant team leader, radio operator, medic, and demolition man. They would recover dead and wounded from downed helicopters, control fire support from the ground, and destroy the aircraft with demolitions, with the squads providing security.

Reconnaissance project organization

The special reconnaissance projects called for small teams capable of independent operations deep in enemy controlled areas. They also required small, flexible reaction forces to aid RTs in trouble or to swiftly exploit targets of opportunity discovered by the RTs.

When Project DELTA was formed in 1964 it consisted of only six reconnaissance/hunter-killer teams composed of four USSF and six LLDB NCOs (some RTs had two USSF and eight LLDB). This proved to be too large for covert reconnaissance. The Montagnard-manned, three-company 91st Airborne Ranger Battalion was attached as a reaction force when activated on November 1, 1964. A fourth company was added in 1965. This was the only airborne Ranger battalion in the ARVN and was under direct LLDB command. In November 1966 it was purged of Montagnards, made all-Vietnamese with six companies, and redesignated 81st Airborne Ranger Battalion. Four companies supported DELTA and two were under LLDB High Command control. Over the next two years DELTA grew with a Strike-Recondo Platoon of 12 teams, each with three USSF and three LLDB. The teams were reduced to three USSF and three LLDB and expanded into 16 RTs. The Roadrunner Platoon had six and later 12 four- or five-man teams of handpicked CIDG. There was also a Headquarters Section of 31 USSF and 50 LLDB, a 124-man Nung Security Company, and a Bomb Damage Assessment Platoon with four USSF and 23 CIDG. B-52 also employed a 200-person civilian work force at its Nha Trang compound and part of it would accompany DELTA when it established FOBs.

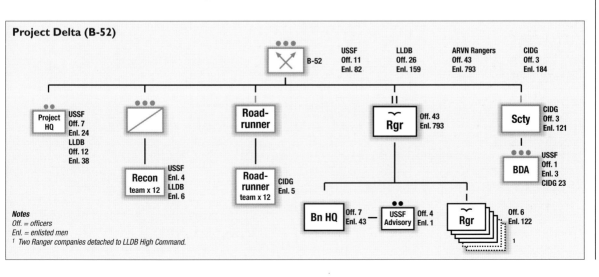

Project Delta (B-52)

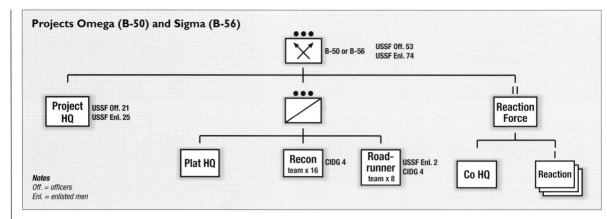

Projects Omega (B-50) and Sigma (B-56)

B-50 or B-56 — USSF Off. 53 / USSF Enl. 74

Project HQ — USSF Off. 21 / USSF Enl. 25

Plat HQ

Recon — team x 16 — CIDG 4

Road-runner — team x 8 — USSF Enl. 2 / CIDG 4

Reaction Force

Co HQ

Reaction

Notes
Off. = officers
Enl. = enlisted men

Projects SIGMA and OMEGA were organized along similar lines to DELTA, but were different in several respects. There was no LLDB participation and while it was originally envisioned to provide each project with an LLDB-controlled airborne ranger battalion, this was not done. Instead, CIDG-manned and USSF-led, three-company MIKE Force battalions were assigned. At their height SIGMA and OMEGA were each authorized 127 USSF and 894 CIDG. Both projects consisted of an expanded B-team operating a Headquarters Section, a Reconnaissance Platoon with eight USSF headquarters personnel, eight roadrunner teams of four CIDG, and 16 RTs of two USSF and four CIDG. OMEGA's indigenous personnel were Jeh, Rhade, and Sedang Montagnards. SIGMA was manned mostly by Cambodians, but Nungs staffed the security company[6] and one of the reaction force companies.

RTs, whether composed of four USSF and six LLDB (early DELTA) or two USSF and four CIDG, adjusted the number of personnel committed to missions. The American team leader was designated the One-Zero, the assistant team leader

---

[6] There is no mention of a security company in OMEGA, possibly because Ban Me Thuot was well protected by other units.

Project DELTA
Special Forces Operational Detachment B-52
Headquarters Section
Strike-Recondo Platoon
Platoon Headquarters
Reconnaissance Team (x12)
Roadrunner Reconnaissance Company
Company Headquarters
Roadrunner Team (x12)
Security Company
Company Headquarters
Rifle Platoon (x3)
Mortar Platoon
Bomb Damage Assessment Platoon
81st Airborne Ranger Battalion
Battalion Headquarters
USSF Battalion Advisory Section
1st–6th Airborne Ranger Companies

Projects OMEGA (B-50) and SIGMA (B-56)
Special Forces Operational Detachment B-50 or B-56
Headquarters Section
Reconnaissance Platoon
Platoon Headquarters
Reconnaissance Team (x16)
Roadrunner Team (x8)
Reaction Force
Battalion Headquarters
1st–3d Reaction Force Company
Company Headquarters
Rifle Platoon (x3)
Weapons Platoon

the One-One, and the radio operator the One-Two, if assigned. The One-Zero was the most experienced and capable man – even if the other less experienced Americans outranked him. The two Americans normally carried their own radios. The senior indigenous was the Zero-One and so on with the second most senior indigenous the Zero-Four or Zero-Six; there were variations in numbering. Six men were generally considered sufficient for security and to carry equipment. In some cases four or five men were committed. The smaller the team, the less likelihood there was of detection. However, smaller teams had less self-defense capability, suffered fatigue sooner owing to more frequent rotation on guard duty at night, and were less capable of fighting their way out of enemy contact. Larger teams were sometimes used when prisoner snatches were conducted – essentially an ambush mission. The six-man team, though, was established in US practice, being used by LRPs and dating back to the World War II Alamo Scouts.

Reconnaissance troops climb 80ft. wire ladders with aluminum-tube rungs into a UH-1H Huey. These allowed reconnaissance teams to be extracted from pick-up zones on which helicopters could not touchdown. The ladders were carried rolled up on the skids and dropped with sandbags attached, to carry them through vegetation.

Weapons and equipment

MIKE Forces mostly used standard US weapons and equipment, but some obsolescent weapons were employed as well those of foreign origin. Being parachute- and helicopter-delivered light infantry that needed to be highly foot-mobile in rugged country and a harsh climate, their armament was light. The same applied to RTs. Their weapons had to provide a great deal of compact firepower in order for a small team to survive engagement. Initially World War II/Korean War-era weapons were employed. These were replaced for the most part by modern weapons in 1968/69.

Weapons

The .30-cal. M2 carbine was the principal shoulder arm of the MIKE Forces and RTs, having been selected as the official CIDG weapon in 1962. It was a light, compact 5.5 lb., selective fire weapon, making it easy to use by indigenous troops. It used a 30-round magazine; 15-round magazines were occasionally encountered. As a selective fire weapon it was to have replaced submachine guns, but it was less than adequate as a primary combat weapon. The automatic rate of fire was 750–775 rpm, far too high for such a light barrel, resulting in overheating. The cartridge was much smaller than that used in rifles and machine guns – no more powerful than a light pistol round. Coupled with a light bullet it had poor knockdown power, range, accuracy at distance, and penetration, especially through dense underbrush and bamboo, which was a serious deficiency. The carbine was originally intended as a personal defense weapon, a more viable alternative to the pistol.

Another primary weapon, on the opposite end of the spectrum, was the .30-cal. M1918A2 Browning automatic rifle. The bipod-mounted BAR was heavy and bulky for an indigenous soldier, but served as the squad automatic weapon. It weighed 19.4 lb. and had a 20-round magazine, which restricted its rate of fire. It had two rates: the commonly used 300–450 rpm and the high rate of 500–650 rpm.

The company machine gun was the .30-cal. Browning M1919A6 light machine gun ("Number 30" was its indigenous nickname). This weapon, too, was heavy, at 32.5 lb. It could be mounted on a 14 lb. M2 tripod, but it was normally used only on its integral bipod. It was fed by a 250-round metallic-link belt, but a gunner usually carried a shorter 50–100-round belt owing to weight. Rate of fire was 400–500 rpm. Many rifle platoon members would carry extra machine-gun ammunition.

In early 1967 the three preceding weapons began to be replaced by first-line models, but it would take over two years to replace all the older weapons. Carbines were turned in for 5.56mm M16A1 rifles, a selective fire 6.3 lb. weapon with a 20-round magazine capable of 650–750 rpm. It was typically used only on semi-automatic to conserve ammunition. While it was compact, light, and allowed a larger amount of ammunition to be carried, the "black rifle" had poor penetration through brush and bamboo and had to be kept meticulously clean. It proved to be a fairly

A mortarman of the 5th MSF poses beside his 60mm M19 mortar in a hasty 6ft.-diameter pit at a forward operations base. Note the use of two-man pup tents. (Lee B. Wilson)

effective weapon, even though the wounds it inflicted were uneven; that is, there were examples of insufficient wounds as well as massive damage. The "CAR-15" submachine gun was a widely used M16 variant. It was not uncommon, though, even into 1968, for units to be armed with a mix of M16 and M16A1 rifles, and M2 and M1 carbines. MIKE Force commanders made repeated requests that they be given priority for M16A1s to standardize weapons and because they were Corps reaction forces. Even when the strikers were armed with carbines the USSF usually had M16A1s, which they had used since the early 1960s.

There was no comparable squad automatic weapon for the M16A1, but the 40mm M79 shoulder-fired, single-shot grenade launcher replaced the BAR. The "thumper" or "blooper" was a compact weapon weighing only 5.95 lb. giving the squad the ability to project high-explosive rounds 150m for point targets and 375m for area fire. The round had a 5m casualty radius. There was also a canister (buckshot) round with a 35m range. Various pyrotechnic rounds (colored smokes and flares) were available. Some RTs modified the M79 by cutting the barrel down by 3in., removing the rear sight, and sawing the butt stock off, leaving a pistol grip. It was carried on a cord or in a canvas holster. This provided a short-range emergency weapon for breaking contact.

The 7.62mm M60 became the new company machine gun (its indigenous nickname was "Number 60"). The bipod-mounted gun weighed 23.05 lb. and had a 600 rpm rate of fire. Ammunition was issued in 100-round metallic-link belts. It had a quick-change barrel to prevent overheating, but a spare barrel was seldom carried.

A few other weapons were occasionally used, mostly prior to 1968: .30-cal. M1 carbine (semi-automatic only), M8 grenade launchers for the carbine, .30-cal. Garand M1 rifle (heavy for indigenous soldiers), and .45-cal. M3A1 submachine gun ("grease gun"). RTs made some use of the Swedish-made 9mm Carl Gustav m/45b submachine gun ("Swedish K"). MGFs used a small number of British Sten 9mm Mk IIS silenced submachine guns. Some use was made of High Standard .22-cal. HD pistols with integral silencers. The standard pistol was the .45-cal. Colt M1911A1. USSF soldiers were each authorized an M1911A1, but few were issued them, let alone carried them in combat. Few were issued to strikers, even if listed on the TOE, owing to the risk of theft. Some CIDG leaders, mainly company COs, were given pistols as a sign of office, a prestige matter.

A US 105mm M101A1 howitzer fires for a II Corps MIKE Force FOB in support of the 4th Battalion, 1969. (Jess Smetherman)

Many RTs armed themselves with Soviet 7.62mm AK-47 (Chinese Type 56) or AKM assault rifles. These rugged, selective-fire weapons used a 30-round magazine and had a 600 rpm rate of fire. There were advantages of carrying AKs. Some RTs wore uniforms to make them appear as NVA/VC and the rifle's distinctive silhouette enhanced this appearance; the sound of an AK firing in enemy-controlled areas would not necessarily cause notice. Enemy ammunition and magazines could be used. A few RTs used the Soviet 7.62mm RPD light machine gun (Chinese Type 56). Weighing only 15.6 lb. and fed by a 100-round belt in a drum, it provided considerable firepower for its size.

The 60mm M19 mortar was the heaviest weapon normally used by MIKE Forces. On the M5 bipod and base plate it weighed 45.2 lb. and had a range of 1,985 yds. The M5 mount could be replaced by an M1 base plate and the mortar fired handheld to a maximum range of 816 yds; as it was fired in this mode with only an ignition cartridge, the propellant charges had to be removed. Its practical range, though, was 350 yds. Minimum range in either mode was 50 yds. In the handheld mode it weighed only 20.5 lb. Some RTs with direct-action missions and reaction forces occasionally used the handheld 60mm, but carried only a few rounds. Ammunition included high-explosive, white phosphorus smoke (WP), and illumination (parachute flare) rounds.

The M72, M72E1, and M72A1 light antitank weapons (LAW) were used against bunkers, buildings, and snipers. This was a single-shot, shoulder-fired, disposable rocket launcher firing a 66mm high-explosive antitank (HEAT) warhead. Its practical range was 170–220 meters, it could penetrate up to 12in. of armor, and it weighed only 5 lb. It sometimes misfired or failed to detonate if striking the target at a low angle, making it a poor weapon against troops in the open. In the early days the 3.5in. M20A1B1 bazooka rocket launcher was used. This 15 lb. weapon fired HEAT and WP rounds to an effective range of 200 yds.

Hand grenades were extensively used including fragmentation, concussion, WP, thermite, tear gas, and colored smoke. The command-detonated M18A1 Claymore directional anti-personnel mine saw wide use in a number of imaginative manners.

Some heavy crew-served weapons saw limited use including the 4.2in. M30 mortar, 81mm M29 mortar, jeep-mounted 106mm M40A1 recoilless rifle, 57mm M18A1 recoilless rifle, and .50-cal. M2 machine gun ("Number 50" was its indigenous nickname).

Equipment

Heavy equipment was minimal for these light forces. The MIKE Force and reconnaissance project detachments were provided small numbers of trucks for administration, logistics, and troop movement. The 2½-ton M35A2 or M135 6x6 cargo trucks ("deuce and a half") could carry 20 or more standing troops. The ¾-ton M37B1 cargo truck was a 4x4 suitable for light utility work. The ¼-ton M151A1 4x4 utility truck[7] ("jeep") was used as a command and liaison vehicle. A variant was the M151A1C, carrying a 106mm M40A1 recoilless rifle.

The numbers of vehicles assigned to a MIKE Force varied. Typically a MSF battalion had two 2½ tons, one ¾-ton, two jeeps, and a 400-gal. (1,514-liter) M149 water trailer ("water buffalo"). These remained at the base and were not taken to the field. (A US infantry battalion had 116 trucks of all types.) The MSF B-team had additional trucks and others might be borrowed from local Free World units for short-distance hauls such as moving troops to departure airfields.

Individual equipment varied widely, being a mixture of standard US web gear from different periods and contract-produced "indigenous" gear made in Asian countries. Specific items carried by MIKE Force strikers and RT

---

7 The M151 is sometimes called the "MUTT" (Military Utility Tactical Truck). This was not an official designation nor was it generally used by soldiers.

Officially a 2½-ton cargo truck could carry 16 troops seated on the side benches. Here the better part of a 5th MIKE Force company is transported. This is an M135 with single rear wheels. The more common M35A2 had dual rear wheels.

A Marine Boeing Vetrol CH-46D Sea Knight cargo helicopter arrives to pick up I CTZ MGF troops bound for Bato. While appearing similar to the Army's CH-47A Chinook, the CH-46 was a smaller aircraft. (Aaron Grtizmaker)

A Marine Sikorsky CH-53A Sea Stallion prepares to load I CTZ MIKE Force troops for lift into their area of operations. Much of the helicopter support provided to the I CTZ was from Marine Aircraft Group 16 at Marble Mountain outside of Da Nang. (Virgil R. Carter)

Two men are extracted using the McGuire rig, named after the inventor, SGM Charles T. McGuire. The rig consisted of four 100ft. ropes each with a 6ft. web strap allowing a man to strap himself in. The man could not be hoisted into the helicopter, but would be flown out dangling below it. (Jess Smetherman)

A 6,000 lb.-capacity rough-terrain forklift hauls a speed pallet dropped from a transport aircraft to a supply dump at a Project OMEGA FOB at Dok To. (Lee B. Wilson)

members varied greatly between units, mission, area, timeframe, and personal preference. During some operations they wore M1 steel helmets and carried entrenching tools, items never carried by camp strikers.

Besides airboats some use was made of "16ft. plastic" M3 assault boats (actually made of fiberglass and 17ft. 8in. [5.4m] long) propelled by 40-hp outboards, which could carry up to 12 men. The RB-3 and RB-15 were three- and 15-man pneumatic boats propelled by paddles, or an outboard in the latter case. Sampans were sometimes used in the Mekong Delta and Montagnard dugouts on rivers. The 4th MSFC in the Mekong Delta was frequently transported by Navy Mobile Riverine Force armored troop carriers, and river and coastal patrol boats.

Aircat airboat

The US tested two airboats during the 1964 and 1965 Mekong Delta wet seasons, the Hurricane Aircat and Susquehanna Skimmer. The Aircat was selected and issued to the 4th MSF and ARVN divisions in the Delta. They saw some use by SF teams in III CTZ in areas bordering the Mekong Delta. The 1,150 lb., 18ft. fiberglass-hulled boats had a speed of 42 knots (48 mph) in deep water, but up to 65 knots (75 mph) over inches-deep rice paddies. They were crewed by two, the operator and gunner, and carried up to five troops. A rifle platoon could be transported in 6–8 boats. The operator sat in the rear just forward of the engine. A .30-cal. M1919A6 was mounted in the bow on an M31C pedestal. On occasion 57mm M18A1 and 106mm M40A1 recoilless rifles, .50-cal. M2 machine guns, and 40mm XM174 automatic grenade launchers were mounted on airboats. Steering was accomplished by an aircraft-like stick, which operated a pair of rubbers aft of the caged 180-hp Lycoming O-360 engine used in Cessna and Piper aircraft. While extremely loud, it was difficult to tell in what direction the airboats were approaching until they were quite close. Their engine noise made on-board radio communications impossible, though. They relied on their impressive speed and ability to maneuver sharply to survive. They carried no armor. Crewmen did not even bother to wear helmets and body armor, although hearing protection was recommended. They could also motor along at very slow speeds with the engine throttled back to a relatively quiet level. Even at slow speeds they drew only inches of water and could skim across mud flats and saturated ground. At high speeds they could bound over rice paddy dykes.

Command, control, communications, and intelligence

Command and control

The 5th SFGA, even though an Army unit, was directly subordinate to MACV rather than US Army, Vietnam (USARV). The Group was headquartered in Nha Trang north of Cam Ranh Bay on the coast of central South Vietnam within II CTZ, and was responsible for all USSF in Vietnam with the exception of those assigned to MACV-SOG. On paper MACV-SOG personnel were assigned to Special Operations Augmentation, 5th SFGA, but in reality they were separate from the Group.

The Group, with progressively increasing numbers of USSF personnel (1,830 in 1965; 3,750 in 1969), superimposed its deployed units over the ARVN regional organization. A USSF company was responsible for all SF units within each corps area. A company, which gives a seriously false impression of the unit's size and responsibilities, consisted of an augmented C-team (company headquarters) and two to four B-teams, each with four or more A-teams. One of the B-teams served as the corps' MSFC. An SF company was commanded by a lieutenant colonel, B-teams by majors (lieutenants colonel in Vietnam), and A-teams by captains. While the companies were deployed from north to south out of sequence (Companies C, B, A and D), their C-, B-, and A-team designations began with the corps number to prevent confusion. Detachments directly subordinate to the Group were numbered in the 5-series (B-50, B-51, B-56, B-57, A-502, A-503) with most under the administrative control of Company E (Provisional) (C-5) at Nha Trang.[8]

Det C-1 (Co C)	Da Nang	CTZ I
Det C-2 (Co B)	Pleiku	CTZ II
Det C-3 (Co A)	Bien Hoa	CTZ III
Det C-4 (Co D)	Can Tho	CTZ IV

The four corps' MIKE Forces were responsible to the C-team, but they could be placed under the operational control (OPCON) of the Group or a US command. This was a common arrangement, for the corps MIKE Force to be OPCON to a US command, but while the US used the ARVN regional organization for convenience, it did not follow it completely. US operational command arrangements were different. The MIKE Forces might have been made OPCON to one of four US corps-equivalent commands. III Marine Amphibious Force was responsible for all US forces in I CTZ including Army. From 1968 Army units in I CTZ were under XXIV Corps, itself under III MAF. I Field Force, Vietnam was responsible for US units in II CTZ, and II FFV was responsible for units in III CTZ. The 5th MSFC usually remained under direct Group control. Regardless of the command assigning a mission to a MIKE Force, the operation had to be approved by 5th SFGA.

Prior to 1969 the II and IV Corps MIKE force battalions were not under centralized C-team command, but under that of some of the different B-teams

---

8 Company E was not assigned an area of responsibility and existed from March 1965 to September 1967. When disbanded the detachments again fell directly under Group control.

and collocated with the B-teams. In April 1969 they were placed under a B-team as an MSFC for centralized control, but remained at their original locations.

An entire MIKE Force was not necessarily assigned to one mission or OPCON to a single command. Different elements could be OPCON or attached to different commands. Most MIKE Force operations were battalion or detached company in size. It was rare that the bulk of an entire MSFC was committed to a single operation. When that occurred, such as in the several operations conducted in the Seven Sisters Mountains region in IV CTZ by 4th and 5th MSFCs, they had to be augmented to provide adequate command and control, signal, and logistical support.

LLDB were assigned to the MIKE Forces in December 1966, although some did not receive any until early the next year. Prior to this MSFs and MGFs were under unilateral USSF command unlike the CSFs who were under direct LLDB command and advised by their counterpart USSF. Only small numbers of LLDB were assigned to an MSF for liaison and they played a very minor role, being virtually excluded from the chain of command. Often they only took part in camp administration and training duties. They had no experience in logistics and were subordinated to the USSF, if not by formal chain of command, by the actual working relationship and their limited authority as recognized by the CIDG. Strikers recognized only American leadership. The few LLDB assigned to MIKE Forces were reluctant to give orders owing to their place and their insecurity among strikers. There was also widespread corruption within the LLDB and their combat proficiency was less than sterling. Battalion-size CSFs were assigned an eight to 12-man LLDB A-team along with a USSF A-team. In 1967 an MSF with three USSF A-teams had only two LLDB officers and four NCOs assigned. More were assigned in late 1967. In August 1968 it was decided to place the MIKE Forces under LLDB command with the USSF acting as advisors. This would be implemented over the next six to eight months. This caused a great deal of concern among the ethnic minority strikers due to demonstrated Vietnamese racial prejudice, corruption, and exploitative practices inflicted on strikers.

An ad hoc field kitchen set-up at a Project OMEGA FOB employed five large rice cookers fired by underground fire pits. Rice would be supplemented by locally purchased fresh chickens and vegetables or canned mackerel and salmon. MIKE Forces used the same kind of facilities. (Lee B. Wilson)

Two 5th MSF Montagnard companies immediately resigned. Regardless of the opposition, LLDB B-teams were assigned to the MSFCs. LLDB B-17 was assigned to the 2d MSFC, for example, but these teams still had little real authority or meaningful participation in operations. In July 1969 B-20 had 22 USSF officers and 75 NCOs while B-17 had 22 LLDB officers and 67 NCOs. There would be a counterpart LLDB A-team for each USSF A-team. Unfortunately a complete listing of LLDB teams cannot be located. Few of the USSF with MIKE Forces even knew what their counterpart A-team's designation was.

Reconnaissance projects too would support US commands. For example, Project OMEGA supported I FFV in II CTZ while Project SIGMA supported II FFV in III CTZ. Project DELTA supported MACV and performed missions for 5th SFGA. DELTA could operate anywhere in the country. Requests for the use of the projects were passed through channels from US divisions and MACV and the field force commander selected which division had the most need. Usually the reconnaissance project was OPCON to a specific division for 30 days. The staff would coordinate with the division and the missions might be conducted anywhere within the division's AO, which might cover up to 2,500 square kilometers. An FOB was established at a C-130-capable airfield, which required about five days. Advanced launch sites (MSS) further from the FOB were set up and it was from the MSS that missions would be launched, supported, and recovered.

Communications

Radio communications was largely handled by the AN/PRC-25 radio, a 24.7 lb. transistorized FM transceiver. This was a back-packed set which came into wide use in 1967/68. It had only a five-mile planning range with its short antenna. A long segmented whip antenna gave it a few more miles, but was so long that it could not be operated while moving. The similar AN/PRC-77 allowed the attachment of an AN/KY-57 secure voice device (cryptographic scrambler), but these were not used in the field, to prevent their capture. It is often assumed that the "Seventy-seven" had a longer ranger than the "Twenty-five," but this was not true.

Preceding the "Twenty-five" was the AN/PRC-10. The "Prick-10" had been in use since the Korean War. It weighed 26 lb. and had a three to five-mile range. While possessing roughly the same range and weight as the "Prick-25," the new radio was more reliable, rugged, easier to operate, and had a broader frequency coverage – 920 channels as opposed to the "Ten's" 170.

In conventional infantry units the "Twenty-five" and the "Ten" were platoon- and company-level radios. In the MIKE Forces they were used at company and battalion levels with each American accompanied by an indigenous RTO (radio-telephone operator). This gave each company typically two radios with three or four at battalion. The battalions would net with the B-team, which may or may not have been in the field. The B-team usually had AN/VRC-46 or -47 radios set up to operate from electrical power generators. These were vehicle-mounted radios carried in the back of a jeep, but could be set up ground mounted in a base camp. In a base the RC-292 antenna ("Two-nine-two") was erected. This was a sectionalized, up to 30ft.-tall mast antenna supported by guy wires. In RTs each USSF normally carried their own radio, either a "Prick-10" or "25."

For intra-company communications the Hallicrafters HT-1 walkie-talkie was employed, with two or three in the company headquarters and one or two in each platoon. This was a civilian AM radio powered by eight D-cell flashlight batteries. It had a telescopic antenna, giving it a range of up to 1¼ miles. Widely used by USSF, it had operating instructions printed in English and Vietnamese. It was provided with a self-destruct button, but this was disconnected as strikers were often curious to see what the red button was for.

A striker cook cleans a serving bowl at a mess kit washstand made from wooden cargo pallets. The 32-gal. GI cans are fitted with immersion heaters that keep the soap and rinse water cans boiling. (Lee B. Wilson)

A specialized radio used by RTs was the AN/URC-10, known as the "Urck-10." This was a pocket-sized, handheld survival radio normally issued to aviators and carried in their survival vests. While the radio was small it used an external battery connected by a cable almost the size of the radio. It was used for emergency contact with extraction helicopters and was especially valuable as it only weighed a few pounds and could be retained even if backpack radios were discarded or no longer operational.

Radios were a heavy addition to everything else a man had to carry. The batteries too were heavy and used up at a high rate. For this reason radios were not normally monitored at company and lower levels. They were turned on for contact when necessary and at predetermined times for scheduled situation reports. RTs typically made three scheduled contacts a day to report their location and situation.

The chief problem with radios was their short range. This was especially critical for RTs, which mostly operated in distant, remote areas. AM single-side band radios using Morse code were heavy, could not be operated on the move, and required long wire antennas to be strung in trees. One such radio, the AN/PRC-74, did see some use by RTs and MGFs. It weighed 24 lb., and was bulkier than the "25," time consuming to set up, and complex to operate. Several techniques were employed to accommodate the radios' short range. Radio relay sites with large antenna arrays, either temporary or permanent, were set up on mountain tops. One example was A-324 atop Nui Ba Den, a 987m (3,228ft.) mountain jutting out of the rolling forests of III CTZ, whose sole mission was radio relay with deployed SF units. UH-1 Huey helicopters fitted with radio consoles and O-1 Birddog observation aircraft would orbit near an RT's operational area and receive transmissions at scheduled times. For critical missions where chances of contact were high a communications aircraft would remain on station being relieved by another after a couple of hours. They could call for and direct air support, gunships, and extraction helicopters. On occasion even tethered balloons at FOBs carried radio relay antennas aloft.

MGFs used HT-1s for intra-platoon communications, the AN/PRC-10 linked platoons and the company headquarters, and the AN/PRC-74 linked the MGF with its base.

Marking one's position on the ground to friendly aircraft was essential, especially when attack helicopters and fighter-bombers were delivering ordnance at "danger close."[9] It was also necessary to mark helicopter pick-up zones for extraction. This was accomplished by a number of means depending on night or day, overhead vegetation, and visibility. Colored smoke grenades, signal mirrors, handheld signal panels, and at night, handheld colored "pop-up" flares, "pen flare" projectors, strobe lights, and flashlights with colored lenses.

Intelligence

MACV operated a complex and highly centralized combined intelligence collection, analysis, and dissemination effort. MACV processed countless intelligence reports from multiple sources – US Army, Marine Corps, Air Force, Navy, the CIA and other civilian intelligence agencies, the Vietnamese armed forces, other Free World forces, and government agencies. When assigned a mission the MSFC would study available information on their assigned AO in an effort to locate possible enemy concentrations, movement patterns, and activities. Order of battle information on enemy unit identification, strength, and armament was also determined.

Reconnaissance projects used the same sources of intelligence as the MIKE Forces, but their most valuable source was their own RTs that had previously operated in the area. In such remote areas under enemy control there were few sources of reliable information available. Airborne sensors, aerial photography, aerial surveillance, and the like were largely unable to penetrate the jungle canopy and enemy camouflage and deception efforts. There were few if any reliable human intelligence sources on the ground. Information from RTs previously operating in the area was the chief and most reliable source of intelligence on terrain, vegetation, enemy roads and trails, enemy dispositions and activities, and water sources.

B-teams, both those of MSFCs and reconnaissance projects, had a captain S-2 (intelligence) officer supported by NCOs and enlisted men. The small S-2 section at C-team level was augmented by military intelligence personnel. The 5th SFGA had a significant intelligence staff with augmentation by ten Military Intelligence detachments: these numbered detachments served only as manpower resources and not as physical units as their personnel were assigned to C- and B-teams and other elements as necessary.

A valuable asset was the highly classified 403d Special Operations Detachment (Radio Research). This was an Army Security Agency (ASA) unit conducting low-level tactical radio and telephone intercept. Field augmentation teams monitored intercept equipment. They had little ability to translate or analyze traffic, so the intercepted recordings were sent to the ASA field station in each corps area. However, CIDG translators were used by some 403d Special Operations Detachment (SOD) teams for immediate translation of critical time-sensitive intercepts.

It was not uncommon for MIKE Forces and RTs to go into enemy-controlled areas with minimal information on the terrain and enemy. Flexibility and the ability to respond effectively to rapidly changing or unexpected situations were necessary. This was gained through Special Forces' approach to training and experience.

Maps were critical to operations. The standard tactical maps used by US forces were 1:50,000 scale with a grid line system of 1,000m squares. Each square was identified by a four-digit grid coordinate number. For more precise

---

9 Doctrinally, "danger close" was when the target was within 600m of friendly positions. Few engagements in Vietnam occurred at 600m. With the precision perfected by aircrews "danger close" in Vietnam was normally considered 200m.

A young IV CTZ MIKE Force striker and a combat interpreter. The striker wears an NVA shirt with the MSF patch, airborne tab, and US jumpwings sewn on. (Jess Smetherman)

coordinates a six-digit coordinate would be used to identify a point within 100m, and for even more precision, an eight-digit to within 10m. Seldom was anything more precise necessary. Distances and elevations were in meters. While updated by US engineers, the maps were based on the original French surveys. In most cases they were fairly accurate, but in the more remote areas, especially in the northern mountains, there were errors in the terrain, with whole ridges and hills sometimes misplaced. Larger streams and rivers, though, were usually accurately placed as the survey lines followed these. The same applied to the main roads, towns, and other major manmade features. Units typically plotted new secondary roads, trails, and significant manmade changes in the terrain.

The evolution of MIKE and special recon forces

Each of the five MIKE Forces evolved organizationally in very different ways, as did the unit designations, drawing on existing security forces, Eagle Flight platoons, separate MIKE Force companies, and MGF companies.

I CTZ MIKE Force

A 148-man Da Nang Nung Reaction Force was organized and trained in July and August 1964 as a reserve to support CIDG camps in I CTZ under B-410, TDY from the 1st SFGA. The unit was expanded to battalion size in November with 560 strikers. In August 1965 A-113 took over the force. It was designated the I CTZ MIKE Force in January 1966. The strength of the force varied widely

Rhade Montagnard strikers of the I CTZ MIKE Force at Ta Bong Strike Force camp preparing to search for missing USSF personnel. One striker wears a gold/yellow on black MIKE FORCE tape over his right pocket. (Virgil R. Carter)

The A-113 MGF at Lang Vei camp (which was later overrun by the NVA) receive a resupply drop using two G-11 cargo parachutes. (Virgil R. Carter)

I CTZ MGF troops aboard a
Marine Corps CH-46D Sea
Knight inbound to a landing zone.
(Aaron Grtizmaker)

I CTZ MIKE Force troops take a
break beside a bamboo grove. While
tiger-stripe boonie hats were issued,
many individuals purchased civilian
made patterns of varying designs.

Strikers cross a rushing stream
in I CTZ. Streams were frequent
obstacles in Vietnam and it was
not uncommon for several to be
crossed in a day's move. The June to
October wet season, or southwest
monsoon, led to the occasional
striker being drowned in a rain-
swollen stream.

at times, being down to 200 troops owing to casualties and desertions. By June 1966 it had been built back up to a guard and three strike companies. In August the 1st–3d Companies were redesignated A–C. In September 1966 Companies B and C and part of A-113 were detailed for an unconventional warfare mission with the USSF reassigned to the provisional A-100. The MIKE Force was soon reconsolidated. In December 1966 the two companies were redesignated 11th and 12th, and a CRP was added.

In January 1967 A-100 established a new unit, MGF 768, with two companies (1st and 2d) and two CRPs manned by Montagnards. In May, after commencing an operation, the strikers refused to continue the mission for unreported reasons. All were dismissed and the MGF disbanded. By August 1967 the MSF had grown to a Headquarters Company (Nung) and 11th (Nung), 12th (Montagnard), 14th (Vietnamese – 13th Company was redesignated 14th), 15th (Nung and Vietnamese), and 16th (Montagnard) Companies, totaling 800 men.

In February 1968 the 12th Company was largely destroyed at Lang Vei (see Campaign 150: *Khe Sanh 1967–68*). It was redesignated the new 15th Company and rebuilt. In February A-111 was assigned to the MSF with the existing A-113. There was no B-team assigned and CO, A-113 remained the MSF commander, which was anticipated to be increased to eight companies. B-16 was assigned to the MSF in May and it was redesignated the 16th MSFC in June. The A-teams were redesignated A-161 and A-162, plus A-163 was assigned in October. Its LLDB counterpart was B-21. Owing to continuing recruiting problems only five companies (the 111th, 112th, 113th, 121st, and 122d) could be maintained and no battalion structure was established. The A-teams essentially lost their identities and were divided up among the companies.

On January 11, 1970 the USSF personnel were withdrawn and the MSF was turned over to LLDB control. The companies were reassigned to former understrength Strike Force camps, being converted to Border Rangers, and the MSF was closed on November 14.

II CTZ MIKE Force

The II CTZ reaction force began to be formed in July 1965 by A-219 under C-2 at Pleiku. Training at Doc Co began in August and lasted through November, but it actually began conducting operations in September. The four-company MIKE Force comprised fewer then 300 Nungs of an authorized 748-man battalion. The Eagle Flight Detachment was absorbed by the MIKE Force at the end of 1965 as a CRP. Through much of 1966 the II CTZ MIKE Force fielded only the 2d and 3d Companies, the 40-plus-man Eagle Flight, and a security platoon. A new 1st Company (Nung and Vietnamese, a first) was raised in August. That same month the 3d Company was given parachute training. In November the 4th Company was raised. In December the Eagle Flight was broken up into four CRPs called Eagle 1–4 with one attached to each company. Initially the Eagle platoons were only squad strength. Strength at this time was 700 strikers.

In January 1967 A-217 was assigned and the companies redesignated 21st–23d, each with an Eagle platoon, plus MGFs 876 (A-218) and 777 (A-217). The MGFs' CRPs were also called Eagle platoons. In March, much of the MSF became parachute qualified with the other companies trained later in the year. In April the two MGF companies were redesignated 24th and 25th MSF Companies and A-217 and A-218 were reassigned to the MSF, increasing USSF for leadership positions throughout the MSF. They still conducted MGF-type missions. The 26th and 27th Companies were formed in July and a training company in August, which provided both basic and parachute training. In November, B-20 was assigned along with a small number of AATTV advisors. The 28th Company was raised in November with CIDG strikers from Project OMEGA and there were now 1,300 troops. The 29th Company was formed in December.

Company 233, 3d Battalion, II CTZ MIKE Force fords a rain-swollen stream. Three 7.62mm M60 machine guns can be seen in this picture. (Sam Wheeler)

In April 1968 the companies were redesignated 201st–209th. The battalion organization was implemented in August with the 1st Battalion's companies designated 211th–213th, 2d Battalion's as 221st–223d, and 3d Battalion's as 231st–233d. In August the Reconnaissance Company was formed and additional AATTV warrant officers attached. On April 1, 1969 the 20th MSFC assumed responsibility for the 4th and 5th MSF Battalions.

B-24 in Kontum was authorized a MIKE Force company in February 1968, the 27th MSF Company. In August it was redesignated the 261st and the 262d MSF Company was raised under A-204. They were joined by the 271st MSF Company assigned to B-22 at Qui Nhon in February 1969, which was redesignated the 263d. These became the 4th MSF Battalion and were reassigned to 20th MSFC in April. The companies had been redesignated the 241st–243d in March.

The II CTZ MIKE Force compound in Pleiku. The double-width long building in the center is the striker mess hall. The USSF quarters are the elongated L-shaped building to the right. Headquarters, supply, dispensary, and administrative buildings occupy the compound's lower right. (Paul Francoeur)

An ad hoc MIKE Force was established under B-23 at Ban Me Thuot in January 1968 with the attached 24th/204th MSF Company and the locally raised 251st and 252d MSF Companies with A-223. Later in the year the 253d Company was formed after the 204th left. In late 1968 the B-23 MSF was designated the 5th MSF Battalion, but remained subordinate to B-23. It was reassigned to 2d MSFC and moved to Pleiku in April 1969, was rebuilt at the MSF Training Center at An Khe, and parachute trained at Pleiku. The 4th and 5th Battalions' A-teams did not change their numbers to coincide with B-20's. With five battalions the II Corps MIKE Force was the largest.

The understrength 5th Battalion was disbanded in December 1969 and a second reconnaissance company was raised. The reconnaissance companies were designated the 1st and 2d. The 1st Company was inactivated in April 1970 with its personnel reassigned to the 1st Battalion and the 2d Company inactivated in May and the troops reassigned to the 4th Battalion. On May 31, 1970 the seven remaining companies converted to Regional Force companies under ARVN control. It continued to conduct operations under USSF until June, though.

The 4th Battalion, II CTZ MIKE Force returns to its base. A green smoke grenade has been popped at the gate, a common celebratory gesture. (Jess Smetherman)

The 4th Battalion, II CTZ MIKE Force base camp at Kontum. The simple quarters are squad huts. More commonly platoon barracks were provided. (Jess Smetherman)

III CTZ MIKE Force

The first III CTZ MIKE Force was formed in November 1964 under A-302 at Bien Hoa with four or five companies. Few records remain of its early activities. The earlier units had been Nung, but with the expansion to the 36th MSFC it recruited mostly Cambodians.

The 36th MSFC was established in May 1968 when B-36 was formally authorized. B-36 (Provisional) had previously run Special Task Force RAPID FIRE, a special reconnaissance operation for II FFV from August 1967. B-36 absorbed MGF 957 (A-303) and MGF 966 (A-304) along with the MSF companies under A-302, two of which had been serving as the RAPID FIRE reaction force. RADID FIRE was disbanded at that time. The first Cambodian MGF, 957, had been raised in October 1966 and MGF 966 in early 1967.

B-36 was assigned A-361, A-362, and A-363 with the 1st–3d MSF Battalions, sometimes referred to as 361st–363d MSF Battalions. The companies were designated 31st–39th. There was also a Reconnaissance Company. In about August 1968 the battalions and companies were redesignated as follows: 31st Battalion (311th–313d Companies), 32d (321st–323d), and 33d (331st–333d). From mid-1969 the battalions were redesignated 1st–3d.

During the latter half of 1970 the 3d MSFC began training battalions airlifted from Cambodia. It trained three at a time to be returned to fight the Khmer Rouge. At the same time, part of the MIKE Force was sent to Cambodia to become the Presidential Guard and was destroyed by the Khmer Rouge. The 3d MSFC was closed down on 1 January 1971 with its seven remaining companies converted to Regional Force companies. B-36 remained to train Cambodians and provided the beginning of US Army, Vietnam Individual Training Group (UITG)[10] on 7 November 1970 as the Long Hai Training Battalion. It was closed on 30 November 1972. Some AATTV served in UITG/FANK.

NCOs of the 3d MSFC examine captured German World War I 7.9mm Spandu MG.08 water-cooled machine guns recovered from a cache. Such weapons were provided to the VC by the USSR from captured German World War II stocks. The 3d MSF had a reputation for uncovering caches. The 3d wore a red, white, and blue scarf.

10 In May it was redesignated the Forces Armée Nationale Khmer Training Command (FANK).

IV CTZ MIKE Force

In February 1966 A-430 opened Camp Don Phuc and established a MIKE Force battalion with the 1st–3d Companies comprising Nungs and Cambodians. It was redesignated A-401 in April 1967 and its companies were soon redesignated 41st–43d. The adjacent 192d Regional Force Company provided base security. In early 1969 the battalion was assigned to B-40, the new 4th MSFC, along with LLDB B-19. A-431 and A-432 were established at To Chau in February and March 1967 to organize MGFs. In July 1967 they were redesignated A-402 (MGF 399) and A-403 (MGF 489) at To Chau. A-402 was relocated to Moc Hoa and A-403 to Can Tho in March 1968. Prior to that A-402 and A-403 operated as a single entity. On October 15 they were placed under B-40 as the 4th and 5th MSF Companies. The three-battalion structure was established with A-401, A-402, and A-403 aligned with each. The MSF companies were designated 41st--51st with three or four companies per battalion. The companies were assigned at random to battalions and not necessarily in numeric order. The 50th–52d Companies were Vietnamese under LLDB command and attached to different battalions. The 1st Battalion was located at Don Phuc, 2d Battalion at Moc Hoa, 3d Battalion at Can Tho with B-40, and the Airboat Company with A-404 at Cao Lanh. The Airboat Company, organized in June 1968, supported all three battalions as necessary. Airboats had been in use since 1966, being assigned to the different MSF units. In November 1968 A-405 was activated at Ha Tien to form the Reconnaissance Company. In early 1969 the companies were redesignated the 1st–9th with some earlier companies disbanded. The 4th MSFC was about 80 percent Cambodian; the rest were Vietnamese and Nungs.

A 3d MSF striker carries a load of 7.62mm SKS carbines found in a large cache near Rang Rang 50 miles north of Saigon, one of the largest caches found with over 3,000 small arms and numerous crew-served weapons, in December 1969. To the right a striker holds the barrel of a 12.7mm DShKM38/46 machine gun.

The four remaining MSF companies (1st Company, 1st Battalion and all of 3d Battalion) were converted to Regional Force companies when the 4th MSFC was disbanded on 31 May 1970.

5th MIKE Force

The origins of the 5th MIKE Force can be traced to the Nung Special Forces Operations Base (SFOB) Security Platoon established for the 5th SFGA SFOB at Nha Trang in early 1964. It was led by USSF NCOs from the 5th SFGA Headquarters. It grew to a company and in November 1964 the Nung Security Force was expanded to a Headquarters Company (the original company with three guard platoons, a CRP, and a weapons platoon) and 1st and 2d MSF Companies in November 1965. A-503 was organized to control the new Nha Trang MIKE Force, the name it was commonly known by throughout its existence. Because of it being located "next to the flagpole" of the 5th SFGA, its priority on personnel and equipment, and the publicity it received, the 5th MSF was commonly known as the "Palace Guard." In March 1966, after the 1st Company was almost wiped out and the 2d Company resigned after the Ashau Camp battle, the MIKE Force was rebuilt. The remaining Nungs were organized

Graduation day for the first 5th MIKE Force parachute class at its Nha Trang base. (Scott Whitting)

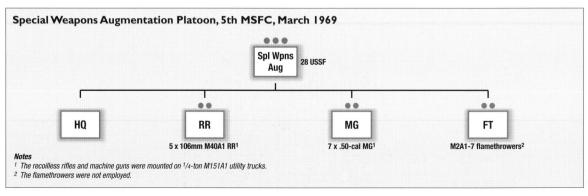

Special Weapons Augmentation Platoon, 5th MSFC, March 1969

```
                              ● ● ●
                          ┌───────────┐
                          │  Spl Wpns │  28 USSF
                          │    Aug    │
                          └───────────┘
        ┌──────────────┬──────────────┼──────────────┐
      ● ●            ● ●            ● ●            ● ●
  ┌─────────┐    ┌─────────┐    ┌─────────┐    ┌─────────┐
  │   HQ    │    │   RR    │    │   MG    │    │   FT    │
  └─────────┘    └─────────┘    └─────────┘    └─────────┘
              5 x 106mm M40A1 RR¹   7 x .50-cal MG¹   M2A1-7 flamethrowers²
```

Notes
[1] The recoilless rifles and machine guns were mounted on 1/4-ton M151A1 utility trucks.
[2] The flamethrowers were not employed.

into a headquarters and service company with a weapons, a security, and two special (role unknown) platoons. From April 1966 three Montagnard companies were raised and by September three more were formed. Two companies rotated as reaction forces for Project OMEGA with B-50 until it was absorbed into MACV-SOG and all companies went through parachute and airmobile training. In late 1966 two CRPs were assigned to the H&S Company. In February 1967 A-503 was placed under Company E (Provisional), 5th SFGA. In September 1967 B-50 relocated to Ban Me Thuot and the 1st–3d Companies went with it. LLDB A-126 was attached for liaison. The 7th and 8th Companies were organized in September and October, respectively. In March 1968 B-55[11] was organized with A-503 taking over the 1st Battalion and A-551 (redesignated

---

11 B-55 had previously been the Command Liaison Detachment (CLD) located in Saigon to coordinate 5th SFGA activities with MACV since October 1964. It remained as the unnumbered CLD.

Two USSF NCOs of the 5th MSFC in 1969 are accompanied by a striker radio-telephone operator carrying an AN/PRC-25 radio. The 5th MSF frequently wore steel helmets. The NCO to the left carries an XM177E2 submachine gun and the other NCO and the RTO M16A1 rifles.

Strikers of the 5th MSF return by air transport to Nha Trang after completing Operation SEAFLOAT in the Delta, where they secured a Navy Mobile Riverine Force base and conducted offensive operations in August and September 1969.

A-504 in June) in the 2d. The companies were designated 511th–513th and 521st–523d and the CRPs organized into a three-platoon Reconnaissance Company. The companies OPCON to OMEGA were permanently separated from the MIKE Force at that time. LLDB B-22 with A-126 and A-176 were assigned in August. For the March 1969 Nui Coto assault a 28-man Special Weapons Augmentation Platoon was organized using volunteers from the 5th SFGA Headquarters, most of whom were support personnel and not Special Forces qualified.[12] In mid-1969 a platoon of two 105mm M101A1 howitzers was organized to support operations in remote areas. In October 1969 the LLDB took over command of the MIKE Force and the USSF became only advisors. The 5th MSFC was disbanded on December 31, 1970. It was not converted to another unit, but apparently the personnel were reassigned to Regional Force units on an individual basis.

Project DELTA

Project LEAPING LENA was established on May 15, 1964 for USSF to train LLDB teams for a reconnaissance mission into Laos. Five eight-man teams were parachuted into Laos in June and July; only five men survived. Other than providing training there was no US participation or control. On July 12, 1964 B-110 and A-111 on TDY from the 1st SFGA arrived to take over the training mission. LEAPING LENA was redesignated Project DELTA in October 1964. DELTA would be under American control and USSF would participate in operations alongside the LLDB. The main base was established at Nha Trang and half of the A-team was at Dong Ba Thin to train the 91st Ranger Battalion (later 81st) as a reaction force. Relations with the LLDB were strained with many quitting as the training was too demanding. Extensive parachute training was undertaken based on the original LEAPING LENA concept of infiltration. A number of LLDB mutinied and the USSF teams were broken up. USSF manning was then provided by other TDY teams from the 1st and 7th SFGA and the year was spent training reliable LLDB and the Rangers. In July 1965 B-52 was organized to manage the project. DELTA's task was to conduct special reconnaissance missions throughout Vietnam for MACV. Over the next two years DELTA expanded greatly, conducting missions mainly in the central and northern portions of the country. Besides reconnaissance missions, in one

---

12 The SWA platoon was armed with 106mm recoilless rifles and .50-cal. machine guns mounted on jeeps plus flamethrowers – it was dubbed the "Super Rat Patrol."

UH-1H Huey helicopters inbound returning a Project OMEGA reaction force company to their FOB. The helicopter crews have wired colored smoke grenades to the rear of their skids and popped them as they approached. (Lee B. Wilson)

instance DELTA and two of its 81st Ranger companies reinforced Camp Plei Me in II CTZ during a bitter NVA siege in October 1965. In September 1966 B-52 established the MACV Recondo School. DELTA successfully conducted hundreds of missions until it ceased operations on June 30, 1970 and B-52 was inactivated on July 31.

Project OMEGA

This project was established in August 1966 at Ban Me Thuot under B-50 and later Kontum. On September 1 it was placed under the command of MACV and tasked to support I FFV to conduct reconnaissance missions in the II CTZ. On November 1 1967 the project was absorbed into MACV-SOG's Command and Control Central. B-50 was inactivated in June 1972.

Project SIGMA

Project SIGMA was formed in August 1966 under B-56 at Ho Ngoc Tau south of Saigon. Like OMEGA it was placed under MACV on September 1 to provide special reconnaissance for II FFV in the III CTZ. On November 1, 1967 SIGMA was absorbed into MACV-SOG's Command and Control South at Ban Me Thuot. B-56 was inactivated on 2 May 1971.

From November 1966 the US Army's 334th Assault Helicopter Company (Callsign "Sabers") was placed under OPCON of the 5th SFGA to support reconnaissance projects. Other US Army and Marine Corps helicopter units were also employed for RT insertion and extraction.

Combat operations

The MIKE Forces conducted thousands of operations during their less than six-year existence. Most of these were small-scale, routine operations, which would be all but impossible to even summarize. Surviving after-action reports are seldom accompanied by maps and the written descriptions of the actions are often unclear on unit routes, positions, and so forth. As a consequence, the maps that accompany this chapter mainly serve to depict what the terrain was like in the area of operations.

I Corps Mobile Guerrilla Force

A good example of an MGF mission was Operation OCONEE or BLACKJACK 12 conducted from March 31 to April 19, 1967. The mission was to locate and interdict VC infiltration routes, determine the VC's strength and future intentions, and direct air strikes on VC installations in an area known as "Happy Valley." MGF 768 under A-100 consisted of eight USSF, four Australians, and 160 CIDG. It was accompanied by a I CTZ MSF company (records do not provide its designation) of six USSF, five Australians, and 176 CIDG. The role of the MSF company was to provide support in the event that contact was made upon insertion, and was part of the deception plan. The two companies boarded Marine CH-46 helicopters at Marble Mountain airfield at Da Nang East at 1545 hours on March 31. They were inserted without incident at 1840 hours, promptly moved short distances, and set up RONs. The next day the two companies moved out, remaining separated by several hundred meters. During the day, five MSF CIDG were "medevac-ed" owing to heat exhaustion and three MSF strikers deserted. On April 2 the MSF company was just over a kilometer to the east of the MGF and was extracted by helicopter at 1330 hours. This was part of the deception plan, hoping to mislead the enemy into believing the entire force had been extracted. The MGF continued westward into increasingly difficult terrain.

An Australian WO and a platoon leader of a Koho Montagnard company, I CTZ Mobile Guerrilla Force during Operation OCONEE. The WO and his Koho counterpart carry HT-1 handheld radios. (Arron Gritzmaker)

Continuing west on the 4th, contact was made with two VC, resulting in one VC killed and one wounded, who escaped. One USSF and two CIDG were lightly wounded. On the 5th thousands of empty NVA ration packets were found along a trail. Later an NVA company was detected to the north and a VC platoon to the south. The enemy was not engaged so as not to give away the MGF's location, and the fear was they might have been in the process of being surrounded. Three VC engaged the MGF's rear platoon and withdrew east; no casualties were suffered on either side. In the late afternoon the MGF received its first napalm container-delivered resupply, but could not locate all containers.

The next morning the remainder of the supplies was located. At 1510 hours an O-1E forward air controller crashed to the south; the rest of the day was spent moving to the crash site and recovering the two bodies. On the 7th the MGF continued west and picked up VC radio transmissions, which made no reference to the MGF's presence. The MGF split up into three elements to scout the area and a helicopter

picked up the flyers' bodies and one of the earlier CIDG wounded. The three elements linked up on Hill 864 on the 8th. The vegetation was so dense that trails had to be used. Upon arrival on the hill the MGF received heavy automatic fire. The VC withdrew to the southwest and air strikes were called in. An MGF patrol detected a VC platoon to the south and engaged it, resulting in three VC wounded. No further contact was made until the 14th when civilians were seen – thought to be guides, trail-watchers, and farmers helping the VC. On the 15th three contacts were made with four to five-man VC patrols. No casualties were suffered by either side. The next day no contact was made. On the 17th patrols were sent north, northeast, and west with the latter engaging two VC squads, twice, again with no casualties.

On the 18th patrols were again sent to the north, northeast, west, and south. The south patrol detected a large group of VC that night. More patrols were sent out and a flare ship was called for, though there was no further contact. Moving north on the 19th the MGF ran into a dug-in NVA platoon, and one Australian was killed and three CIDG wounded. The MGF withdrew from the ridge and at noon two NVA platoons attempted to flank

An XM177E2 submachine gun-armed I CTZ MIKE Force NCO searches the entrance of a tunnel concealed at the base of a cliff, 1967. (John E. Judy)

A water point in a fire support base among heavily constructed sandbag bunkers at Fire Support Base Stainless Steel near Nui Coto. Suspended from the tripod is a 36-gal. canvas Lister bag with six spigots for filling canteens. (William J. Boggs)

them. Air strikes were directed resulting in 35 enemy dead, plus another 27 were killed by the MGF. It was now obvious that the enemy was moving large forces in towards the MGF. Owing to fatigue after 20 days and the amount of enemy movement detected by aircraft it was decided to extract the MGF. This was accomplished from 1810 to 1850 hours with one helicopter door gunner wounded.

The MGF had lost one dead and eight wounded, while they had killed 63 enemy troops (confirmed by US body count). No doubt more were killed and wounded. The operation's assessment confirmed there was a significant VC and NVA presence in the area, that it was being used as an infiltration route, and contained numerous way-stations. No NVA troops in transit were discovered, those encountered appeared to be base support troops, and no evidence of rockets was found. It was considered a successful operation and the VC/NVA no longer felt secure in this base area.

I Corps MIKE Force

The MIKE Forces conducted countless small-scale, short-duration missions. The example that follows is a typical one. Operation ROBIN HOOD was conducted from December 6 to 13, 1968 in the vicinity of the Minh Long Strike Force Camp (A-108). A company from this camp participated in the operation with three I Corps MIKE Force companies (121st and 122d, while 113d served as the reaction force) and two companies from Camp Ba To (A-106) to the south. The AO was northeast of Ba To in the Song Na river valley. NVA were transiting the area via trails toward Quang Ngai City. It was reported that the 2nd Regiment, 3rd NVA Division was moving into the area from Laos to attack Camp Ba To. The NVA were supported by a local VC company. The three MSF companies were each manned by 102–104 CIDG, two to three USSF, two to three LLDB, and two interpreters. The 121st and 122d Companies both established a series of bases from which patrols were dispatched to sweep the area.

The three camp strike companies had established blocking positions to the northwest of the MSF companies. The two MSF companies swept northwest in an effort to drive the NVA from the valley and disrupt their movements and logistics, so that they would abandon their plans to attack Ba To. The NVA refused to be decisively engaged and harassed the MSF movements with two-man sniper attacks. The snipers had well-camouflaged prepared positions and would withdraw to fallback positions as the strikers advanced. The harassing fire was continuous and slowed movement, but striker morale remained high. Their fire discipline, though, was lax and they needlessly expended ammunition. Any enemy structures found were burned. The area had been entirely vacated by civilians. The companies experienced poor

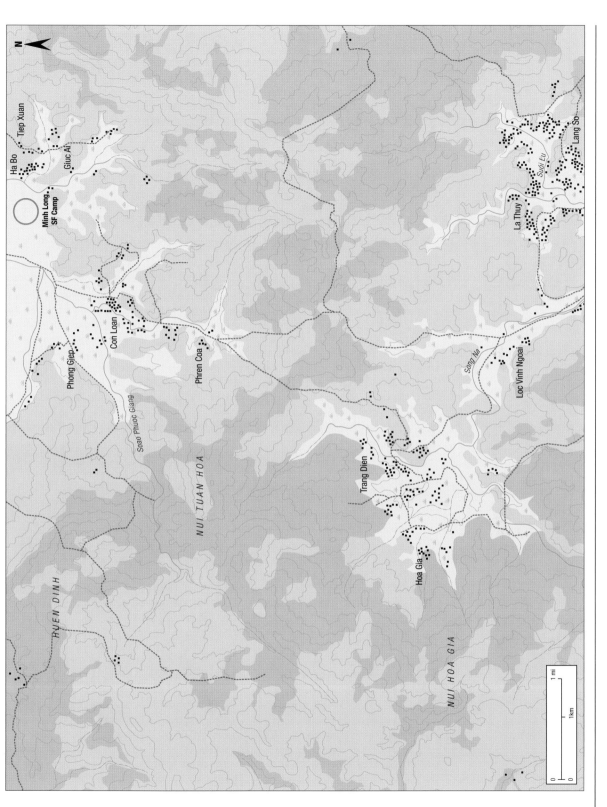

I Corps MIKE Force, Operation Robin Hood, December 6–13, 1968. This area was typical of the terrain in which I CTZ operated, being extremely rugged and with elevations ranging from below 100m to over 800m above sea level. The trees and underbrush on the mountainsides were extremely dense while many of the crests were covered by high grasses. Any level areas in the rare valleys were occupied by rice paddies.

communications when on low ground, but radio relays were usually established via forward air control aircraft. Artillery and air support were adequate, but psychological operations were lacking and could have helped persuade civilians to return to their homes to provide intelligence information and receive medical aid.

The NVA and VC managed to slip past the three blocking companies, but six VC were killed and one captured with four camp strikers wounded; 3,000 lb. of rice were also destroyed. The MSF companies lost five wounded, and one drowned crossing a river. The MSF reported finding no enemy bodies. While results were modest, the attack on Ba To never developed as the operation disrupted NVA plans and they withdrew from the area. By employing only three MSF and three CSF companies against a larger deploying enemy force, the economy-of-force operation forestalled the camp attack and what probably would have resulted in a costly reinforcement and relief effort.

II Corps Eagle Flight

Many Eagle Flight operations were simply reconnaissance and ambush missions. Angel Flight missions to rescue or recover aircrews were also common. Two such missions were conducted in March 1965. The first occurred on March 15 when the Eagle Flight was alerted that a B-57 Canberra bomber had radioed a distress call, having experienced non-combat mechanical problems. As the Eagle Flight boarded its helicopters, the bomber crashed. The Eagle Flight conducted aerial and ground reconnaissance and recovered the body of one crewman. The second was not found. On the last day of the month another Eagle Flight mission assisted in the evacuation of a downed UH-1B helicopter crew. Eagle Flight squads were inserted at points around the helicopter to secure the approaches as one squad assisted the crew onto a rescue chopper. The squad also recovered machine guns, ammunition, radios, and documents from the downed bird. On some missions they would destroy the aircraft with demolitions, but in this instance a CH-37 heavy lift helicopter flew the Huey out. The Eagle Flight squads stayed in the area until this was accomplished while its own helicopters orbited around the crash site some distance out on the lookout for approaching VC. If any were detected they would be engaged, and their presence reported to the ground element. As in so many operations of this type no contact was made with the enemy in either instance. To demonstrate this in July the Eagle Flight conducted 14 combat patrols, 217 reconnaissance patrols, served as a reserve for an ARVN operation, secured an airstrip, and recovered two crewmen from a downed aircraft – all without a single contact. One striker was wounded by a mine, 28 suspected VC structures were burned, and propaganda leaflets were left at former VC sites.

III Corps MIKE Force

Operation BULL RUN I was conducted from August 18 to September 22, 1969 in northeastern III CTZ. Elements of the 5th VC Division were infiltrating into AO KIOWA from Cambodia and it was believed they intended to attack the Duc Phong (A-343) or Bunard (A-344) Camps and/or the Province capital of Song Ba (B-34). The mission of the 3d MSFC was to conduct reconnaissance-in-force and search-and-clear operations; determine enemy activity; map road and trail systems; conduct bomb damage assessments; destroy enemy forces, materials and installations; and divert possible attacks on the suspected enemy objectives. One of the 5th VC Division's regiments and other elements were already in the AO and it was suspected this was the beginning of a build up of the entire division. The MIKE Force battalions would conduct many bomb damage assessment missions during the course of the operation owing to the extensive supporting close air and Arc Light strikes.

The 2d MSF Battalion air-landed at Duc Phong Camp on 18 August to secure the surrounding area, being flown in from its base at Long Hai. The

Reconnaissance Company, Headquarters and Service Company, 361st CSF Company for security; and Battery D, 2d Battalion, 13th Field Artillery (known as the "Jungle Battery," this provisional battery was armed with 105mm and 155mm howitzers) were delivered later and established FOB Maria, which also served as a fire support base. On the 20th the 2d Battalion deployed on foot into AO KIOWA for a reconnaissance-in-force, saturating the eastern section. That afternoon the 1st MSF Battalion closed in on Maria and the next day air-assaulted into AO KIOWA for a reconnaissance-in-force. The same day the first of 13 planned Reconnaissance Company teams was inserted into AO KIOWA. On the 23rd the 3d MSF Battalion air-landed at Bunard Camp to reinforce it and serve as a reaction force.

A reconnaissance team sighted approximately 40 NVA in the afternoon of the 23rd moving west. The 1st Battalion was immediately air-assaulted to exploit targets located by the RT. The 1st Battalion initiated contact with an NVA battalion on the 24th and killed 27 enemy with the loss of four MSF dead and 14 wounded, and one USSF and a US forward observer killed. On the 25th the 3d Battalion was air-assaulted from Bunard with the mission of assisting the 1st Battalion in conducting a sweep of the contact area. The 1st Battalion located an enemy base camp on the 26th that covered several square kilometers. Enemy troops had fled in the past 24 hours and the 1st Battalion continued the sweep. The 1st Battalion also located 60 enemy bunkers in another area, which had been occupied within the past three days. On the 28th the 2d Battalion completed its mission and closed into Maria, in preparation for airlift to Long Hai on the 29th to reorganize and retrain. The 1st Battalion found a small enemy base camp of 23 bunkers on the 31st. It had recently been occupied, and abandoned rucksacks with fresh bloodstains were found. The 1st Battalion continued a sweep of the area and detected an unknown-size enemy force to the northwest. Just before noon the 1st Battalion engaged the enemy. Enemy casualties were unknown and the battalion lost one dead. In preparation for heavy contact the 3d MSFC ordered the 3d Battalion to be air-lifted in to support 1st Battalion. The 3d

Walking wounded of 1st Battalion, 3d MSF are led into a CH-47A Chinook helicopter for mass medevac near Duc Phong Strike Force Camp, September 1969. Both the 1st and 3d Battalions took heavy casualties.

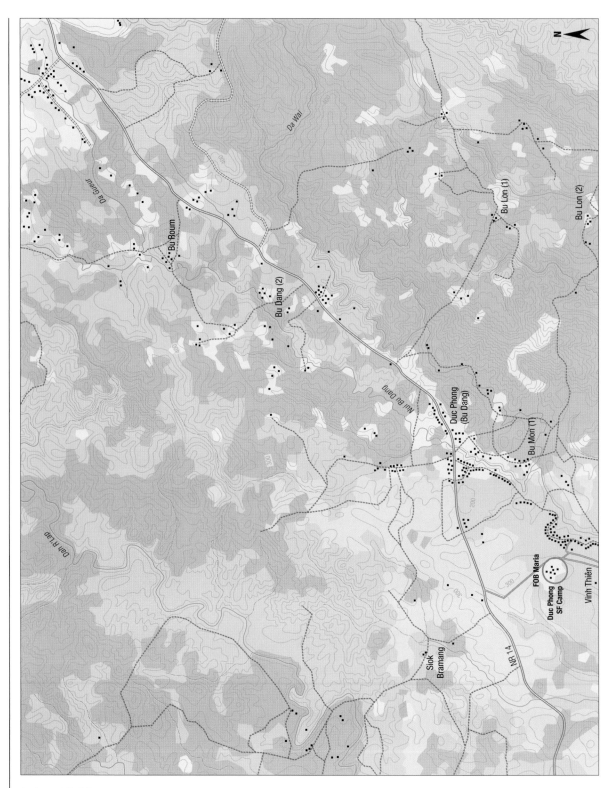

III Corps MIKE Force, AO KIOWA, Operation BULL RUN I, August 18–September 22, 1969. The remoteness of Special Forces camps is demonstrated here by Duc Phong some 30 miles south of the Cambodian border and 80 miles northeast of Saigon. National Route 14 (QL14–Quoc Lo) bisects the area. The terrain comprises rolling hills 270–470m above sea level. To the north of the camp is a rubber plantation while the rest of the area is a mix of single- and double-canopy forest, bamboo, brush, and elephant grass. The many streams were crossable by foot, as this was the dry season, and they provided water to both sides.

Battalion was combat assaulted from its field location five kilometers south in the late afternoon to support the 1st Battalion. In the afternoon 1st Battalion re-established contact with the NVA battalion, resulting in eight MSF wounded. Enemy casualties were unknown. Contact was again made on the same evening with the enemy, who used mortars and machine guns to support a ground attack against 1st Battalion from all sides. The battalion's perimeter was penetrated from the north and it withdrew.

On the morning of September 1 the nearby 3d Battalion was ordered to hold and act as a blocking force for the 1st Battalion. At 1200 hours, a reaction force of 200 CIDG from Duc Phong Camp and 50 Reconnaissance Company troops were air-assaulted into the area in support of the 1st and 3d Battalions. Their mission was to establish a blocking position to the west. With the 1st Battalion to the south, the reaction force to the west, and the river to the east, the 3d Battalion maneuvered from north to south to engage the enemy. At 1420 hours 3d Battalion received heavy mortar and B-40 fire. They broke contact at 1510 hours after suffering ten MSF dead and 30 wounded, and two USSF wounded; enemy casualties were unknown. The 3d Battalion again engaged the enemy at 1605 hours and sustained no additional casualties.

On September 3 the 3d Battalion was hit by a ground attack from all sides. A 200-man reaction force departed Maria and was combat-assaulted in to support the beleaguered battalion. It joined forces with the 1st Battalion to the west. The consolidated force moved in the direction of the 3d Battalion in the late afternoon of the 3rd. At dusk the force reached the 3d Battalion, enabling it to prepare for mass medevac of dead and wounded. All forces were extracted and helicoptered to Maria. The entire 3d MSFC (less the 2d Battalion and B-36 Rear in Long Hai) was now located at Maria. Both battalions had suffered casualties and a B-52 bomber strike was planned for the contact area. In the mid-morning of the 4th the 1st MSF Battalion departed Maria for Long Hai to reorganize. The 2d Battalion at Long Hai was flown back to the FOB.

On the 5th the 2d Battalion began a combat assault into AO KIOWA to conduct a reconnaissance-in-force. Three lifts had inserted elements of the 2d Battalion when a supporting gunship was shot down. Enemy troops were spotted near the downed gunship. The remainder of the 2d Battalion was diverted to the area and the battalion elements already on the LZ were picked up and inserted in the same area. The crew was rescued and the 2d Battalion moved in pursuit of the fleeing enemy. In the afternoon the 2d Battalion made contact. In an hour-and-a-half fight, the enemy left 21 bodies behind. Friendly casualties were two MSF wounded. At 0250 hours on the 6th Maria received a mortar and rocket attack resulting in one dead and four wounded USSF and four wounded MSF. Maria and Duc Phong Camp received an all-night mortar and rocket attack, with only one MSF and two US artillerymen wounded at Maria. On the morning of the 6th the 2d Battalion was air-lifted out of AO KIOWA and returned to Maria to be redeployed to the northern sector for a BDA. The combat assault of the 2d Battalion was canceled by higher headquarters and it remained at the FOB.

On the afternoon of the 10th the 1st Battalion closed into Maria from Long Hai. That same day the 3d Battalion was air-lifted to Long Hai for reorganization and retraining. On the 11th the 2d Battalion was combat assaulted into AO KIOWA to conduct a BDA. In the afternoon the 1st Battalion departed Maria by foot for a reconnaissance-in-force. On the 13th the 2d Battalion was diverted south because an Arc Light strike was postponed 36 hours and there was no need for the battalion to conduct a BDA. On the 12th at 0300 hours Maria sustained a mortar and rocket attack, resulting in one MSF dead and three wounded. That afternoon a gunship picked up a surrendering NVA soldier. On the 15th the 2d Battalion was air-lifted from AO KIOWA and returned to Maria. Before dawn the battalion was hit with mortars, resulting in one MSF dead and one wounded. On the morning of the 16th the 2d Battalion

IV CTZ MIKE Force strikers inside one of Tuk Chup's many caves, which were often interconnected, April 1969. They are testing out the reception of an HT-1 radio, which was ineffective inside caves. (William J. Boggs)

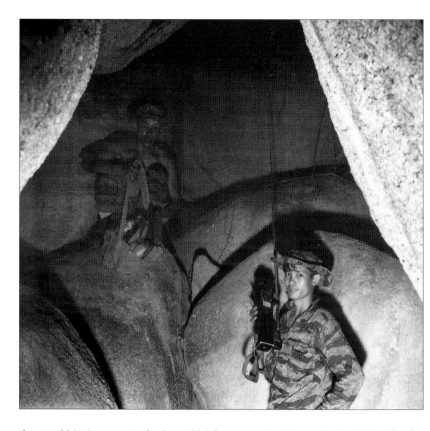

departed Maria en route for Long Hai for reorganization and retraining. On the 16th problems developed when 1st Battalion reported 94 strikers had mutinied and was returned to the FOB on the 18th. Their weapons and equipment were confiscated and they were fired before being flown to Long Hai. On the 17th the 3d Battalion flew back to Maria from Long Hai to prepare to be air-assaulted into AO KIOWA. At 1430 hours the assault was canceled because the 332d and 333d Companies refused to go on the operation, stating they wished to join the Regional Force (which seldom conducted offensive operations). On the 19th the 3d Battalion was persuaded to undertake a foot reconnaissance-in-force mission to the south and east of Maria. The 3d Battalion returned to the FOB on the 22nd. Owing to heavy casualties and desertions plus the building dissent among the strikers, BULL RUN I was terminated on the 22nd. The 1st and 3d MSF Battalions departed Maria at noon. The FOB was closed at 1400 hours on the 24th.

BULL RUN I may not have been a proud moment in the annals of the MIKE Forces, but its mission was accomplished. NVA forces withdrew back to Cambodia and no ground assaults were launched on the targeted camps. Numerous problem areas were uncovered within the MIKE Force. Because of the previous tempo of operations the MIKE Force was unable to sustain its training. With the turnover of personnel no refresher training had been given and the companies were unable to function effectively. The strikers were inadequately trained in platoon and company tactics, battle drill, crew-served weapons employment, assault of fortified positions, movement security, and ambushes. The dissent among the troops, believed instigated by Khmer Kampuchea Krom[13] among the Cambodians, was due to the inadequate level of training, the operation's high tempo, and high casualty rate. In spite of all this, the MIKE

---

13 The KKK was a political organization dedicated to regaining control of the Mekong Delta/Lower Cambodia, which had once belonged to Cambodia.

Force was able to impede the plans of the better-trained and motivated 5th VC Division without the need for US or ARVN units. The entire MIKE Force underwent four weeks of intense training; the 1st Battalion took five weeks to train new recruits. 3d MSFC suffered 28 dead, 181 wounded, and 24 missing (mostly deserters) among the strikers; two USSF dead and ten wounded; one US artillerymen killed and two wounded; and four LLDB wounded. The NVA lost 73 confirmed dead, with more dead probably taken away from the scene and others killed by air and artillery, along with hundreds wounded.

IV Corps MIKE Force

Operation SNAKEMAN II was conducted in Kien Thong and Kien Phong Provinces in northeast IV CTZ from March 20 to April 8, 1968. The 1st MSF Battalion under A-401 deployed an ad hoc force of four drastically understrength companies, 43d (57 men), 45th (47), 47th (25), and 48th (25) with personnel drawn from 11 different platoons. Total strength was 154 CIDG, four USSF, two LLDB, and two interpreters. In spite of the lack of unit cohesion the force functioned to an acceptable standard. The force was tasked with interdicting enemy land and water infiltration routes and conducting search-and-destroy operations against known and suspected VC installations. The operation was launched based on aerial surveillance that discovered considerable activity along the 10km Phuoc Xuyen Canal and frequent small-arms fire from a particular area. Agent reports of infiltration activity reinforced the assessment.

It is interesting to examine the armament of the understrength MSF companies. The 43d and 45th Companies had two small platoons armed with M16A1 rifles and two M79 grenade launchers and a BAR per squad. These companies each had a single M1919A6 machine gun and a 60mm mortar with 20 rounds. The one-platoon 47th and 48th Companies were armed with M2 carbines and, unusually, one 7.62mm M14A1 automatic rifle per squad. There were no M79s or crew-served weapons. These two companies carried two Claymores per squad and the other two one per squad. All troops carried four fragmentation grenades and two colored smoke grenades. The USSF and LLDB carried M16A1s.

A MIKE Force S-2 NCO interrogates a VC prisoner with the aid of an interpreter at Fire Support Base Stainless Steel near Nui Coto, April 1969. (William J. Boggs)

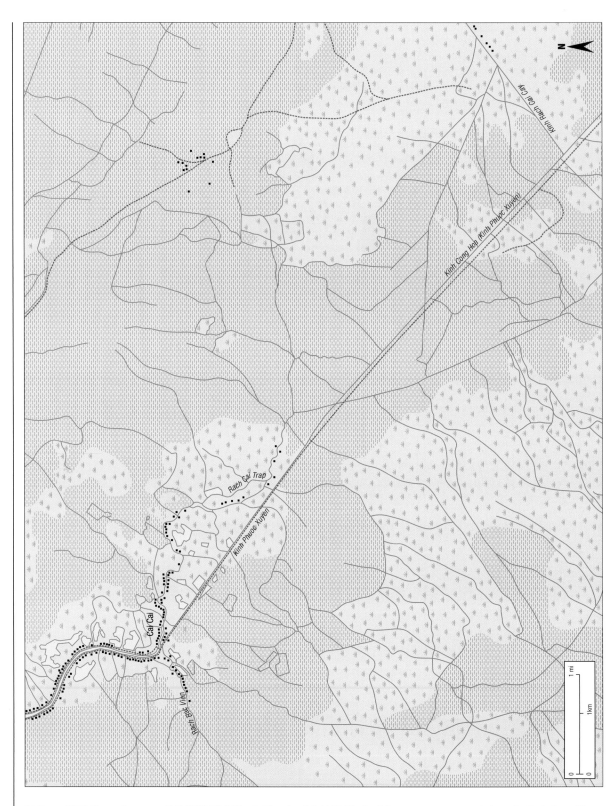

IV Corps MIKE Force, Operation SNAKEMAN II, March 20 to April 8, 1968. Much of the operation occurred along the Kinh Cong Hoa Canal. The Cambodian border lies a short distance to the north. While the Mekong Delta was flat, ground-level visibility was limited owing to high grass and brush. The inundated areas – shown in blue – were dry during the November to April dry season. The many streams and the smaller canals were crossable by foot.

The four MSF companies departed their Don Phoc base on foot, entered the SNAKEMAN AO before noon, and established a patrol base. Two CSF companies at Binh Thanh Thon (A-413) and Cai Cai (A-431) were dedicated as reaction forces. Two houses were found with evidence of mine and booby-trap manufacturing, and were burned. Five VC were spotted before dusk, but withdrew before they were within engagement range. Ambushes were established around the patrol base and every night thereafter.

Patrols were sent out the next day and water traffic on canals was halted and searched; no contraband was found and the crews' papers were in order. Over the next eight days the patrol base was occasionally moved, resupply helicopters were received, patrols swept the area, and civilians were checked. A couple of individual VC were spotted, pursued, and lost. Bunkers, small rice and ammunition caches, and a few VC huts were discovered and destroyed. Two strikers were wounded by booby traps and medevac-ed. On 30 March in the early morning four VC were ambushed and two wounded, according to blood trails. Four hidden sampans were discovered full of food and grenades. In the evening of the 31st two VC platoons were detected and engaged, resulting in four VC wounded and abandoned equipment and ammunition found. That night four VC were ambushed with one killed. During these patrols and ambushes the force would break up into three elements – 43d, 45th, and the tiny 47th and 48th Companies together.

Patrolling continued without contact until the 3rd. That day the three elements linked up and were moving in three files on a parallel route when the right flank was taken under fire by two VC platoons to the right and front. The left file maneuvered to protect the left flank and was engaged from the front, as was the center file. 60mm mortar rounds began to fall among the force and tracers set fire to the high grass in their rear. The enemy to the front was dispersed and began breaking contact. The center file maneuvered to the right to face that threat, fearing the right file would become isolated, but the VC there began breaking contact too. They fled toward the Cambodian border, but the force could not pursue them as they were not allowed within a kilometer of the border. The result was 15 dead VC and four CIDG and one USSF wounded. The wounded were medevac-ed and a new patrol base established. A much-needed ammunition resupply was not delivered until 1400 hours the next day. Ambushes were set with no contacts, but five out-of-range VC were seen in the morning. More ambushes were set on the night of the 4th and a VC squad was ambushed with one VC killed and two wounded. Soon after, VC radio traffic was picked up on an AN/PRC-25 indicating six enemy platoons were north of the ambush site and moving in its direction. The ambush was withdrawn to the patrol base. In the afternoon of the 5th patrols were sent to the south and east to ensure their rear was clear. Then, before dusk, they searched to the north. One patrol engaged four VC, killing one and wounding two. No contact was made on the 6th. The patrol base was moved to the southeast and numerous patrols were dispatched through the 7th without contact, although numerous bunkers and booby traps were found and destroyed.

On the 8th the force was ordered to withdraw and a replacement MSF unit would deploy to continue the mission. The force closed on its Don Phuc base at 1530 hours on April 9. Friendly casualties were one USSF slightly wounded and eight strikers wounded, one seriously. Confirmed VC casualties were 18 dead and 11 wounded with probably more casualties actually inflicted. Twenty-four sampans were destroyed or captured, some 45 bunkers destroyed, and a small quantity of rations and munitions destroyed. A reconnaissance-in-force operation such as this seldom resulted in decisive engagements, but kept the enemy off balance. These operations caused him to disperse his forces, hampered logistics and troop movements, and made it difficult to mass for attacks on Free World installations.

The northeast side of 614m Nui Coto Mountain (Nui means mountain) in northwest IV CTZ. This longtime VC stronghold was the site of many 4th and 5th MSF battles. The rectangular area in the left foreground is Phum Tale, one of many villages surrounding the Seven Sisters Mountains. (William J. Boggs)

5th MIKE Force

Since July 1968 Free World units had been attempting to capture Nui Coto Mountain in the IV CTZ. This is the principal and southernmost peak in the Seven Sisters Mountains straddling the Vietnamese–Cambodian border. In November 1968 the 4th and 5th MSFs had made an effort to capture it, with little success. Three companies of the 5th MSF had jumped in east of Nui Coto to spring a rapid assault, but this had achieved little. For 20 years the VC held this area and prepared sprawling underground fortresses. Artillery, air strikes, and B-52 raids had not been able to dent the stronghold. Much of the surrounding population was of Cambodian ancestry and the VC promised them this area would be re-united to Cambodia after they won the war. This, coupled with the apparent inability of the allies to root out the VC, especially on the 614m Nui Coto, had hampered government attempts to establish authority and pacify the area. The VC boasted their strongholds were

The 238m Tuk Chup Knoll, also known as the "Rockpile," a key VC strongpoint on the southwest side of Nui Coto. The massive pile of boulders was riddled with caves and fortified positions. (US Army)

Nui Coto: 5th MSF troops load captured VC on to a UH-1H Huey helicopter during one of the 1969 operations to subdue the longtime enemy stronghold.

invincible, and after eight months of bitter fighting and hundreds of friendly casualties their boast stood. A semi-detached peak on the northwest side of Nui Coto, 238m Tuk Chup Knoll, had been further christened "Million Dollar Knoll" because of the quantity of allied ordnance fruitlessly expended on it. The area was defended by an estimated 100–150 VC but another 500–600 were available for quick reinforcement from Cambodia. The most heavily defended areas were Nui Coto's southern slopes from the 300m contour line downward and Tuk Chup. Trails and ravines were sewn with mines and booby traps.

The USSF CO of the 2d Battalion and CO of the 6th Company, 5th MSF check a cave entrance on Tuk Chup Knoll, Nui Cuto, March 1969. Both carry their XM177E2 20-round magazines in World War II-era BAR belts. Four 20-round magazines could be carried in each of the six pockets, but grenades or air-ground marker items might be carried in one or two pockets.

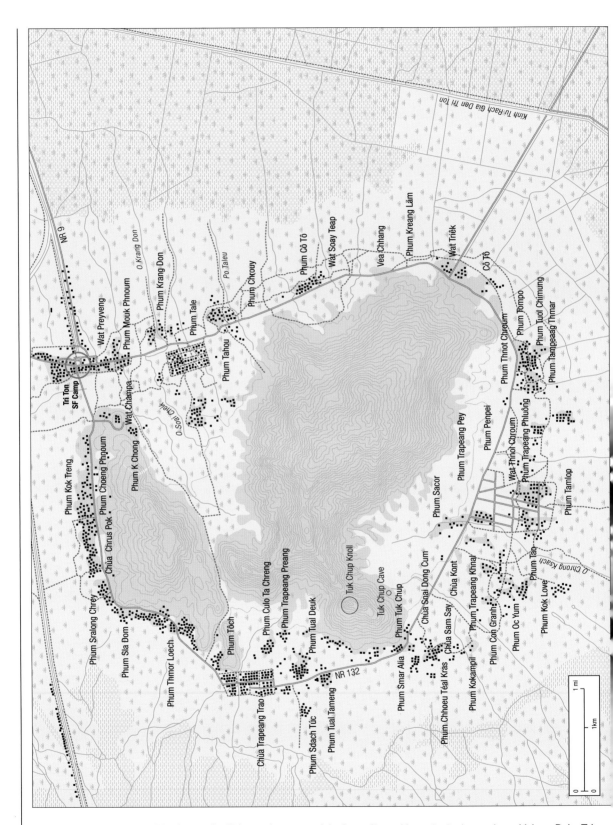

5th MIKE Force's operations. Nui Coto is the 614m southernmost of the Seven Sisters Mountains in the northeast Mekong Delta. Tuk Chup Knoll, the main objective, lay on a semi-detached peak west of the northwest end. Tuk Chup Cave on the southeast slope was a major VC supply point. Drop Zone Monsoon was in the rice paddies just east of the southeast end of Nui Coto.

Strikers and a USSF NCO of the 5th MIKE Force on Nui Coto share a hasty meal of instant rice and canned mackerel, the standard field ration. (William J. Boggs)

Meetings were held during February 1969 among representatives of 5th SFGA, IV CTZ, and 44th Special Tactical Zone, the command responsible for the Seven Sisters Mountains. It was agreed that Nui Coto had to be taken. A three-phase plan was developed. During Phase I, CIDG troops from local Special Forces camps, Regional Force soldiers, and the National Police would cordon off the villages nestling around the mountain. A strong VC infrastructure tyrannized these people and they were coerced into providing food and supplies. Phase I was intended to curtail this flow as well as weed out the local VC and liberate the local population. Phase II called for sealing off Tuk Chup Knoll to isolate the enemy and deny resupply and

A patrol base at the bottom of rocky Tuk Chup Knoll (Chup means knoll). Foot travel up such slopes was treacherous and tiring, plus the enemy could fire from any direction and often chose to attack a MIKE Force unit after it had passed. (William J. Boggs)

reinforcement. The first two phases were designed to weaken the enemy for Phase III when friendly units would storm the knoll, secure it, and clear the VC off the entire Nui Coto mountain.

The 5th MSFC's 1st and 2d Battalions were selected for the assault. The operation commenced on March 4 1969 and by March 14 Phases I and II were completed. By March 15 the 5th MSF had flown from their home base in Nha Trang to positions west of Nui Coto. On March 16 at 0430 hours an artillery barrage commenced. At 0530 the assault began with the MSF companies crossing the surrounding rice paddies. Hidden within their caves enemy gunners waited. The mountain comprised thousands of piled boulders, many larger than a two-story house, and provided formidable cover for VC machine gunners, mortarmen, and snipers. At 0645 hours the enemy opened fire. B-40 rockets, M79 grenades, automatic weapons, and small arms rained down on the attackers. Almost 20 percent of one company became casualties in the first two minutes. It was impossible for friendly troops to tell where the fire was coming from owing to the countless openings among the boulders. In previous attacks Free World units had been defeated by this deadly marksmanship, resulting in Nui Coto being called "Superstition Mountain." Regardless, the 5th MSF pushed up the rock-strewn slopes, clambering over huge boulders, clawing their way up steep paths. The lead soldiers reached the knoll's summit at 0805 hours. There was now a solid line of troops up the west side of Tuk Chup. The plan called for this line to sweep south around the flank and clean out the dozens of caves pivoting on the peak. Past experience had shown the futility of charging the knoll frontally. Allied attempts at heliborne landings on the peak, followed by attacks down the face of the knoll, had also failed.

NCOs of the 5th MSFC at Nui Coto in 1969 call for artillery fire after plotting their location and the target on a map.

The remainder of March 16 and 17 were used to prepare for the flanking sweep. Throughout this period both battalions received constant enemy fire. On the 17th nine VC defected. The MIKE Force's success, coupled with psychological operations, had convinced these troops that this time allied forces were going to take the knoll. The defectors provided valuable information about cave locations and weapons caches. On the 18th the 5th MSF began their sweep around the height, with the 2d Battalion responsible for the upper portion and the 1st Battalion the lower. The three 4th MSF battalions covered the rear to ensure all-around security. In the past the enemy had often waited until an assault line had swept over their positions before popping out of their spider holes and caves and firing on the assault troops from the rear. The assault plan was designed to prevent this and ensure the enemy was always to the front of the attacking troops. In the early afternoon a 1st Battalion company encountered stiff opposition, resulting in heavy casualties. The reserve company moved forward to strengthen the line and the advance continued. Methodically, every cave and possible hiding place was searched and cleared out. The Special Weapons Platoon provided invaluable support using the 106mm recoilless rifle and .50-cal. to place precision fire into narrow openings. Direct 105mm support was provided by Battery B, 6th Battalion, 77th Artillery of the 9th Infantry Division, firing over 14,000 rounds. Progress was slow and tedious. Snipers were a constant threat, although few enemy, dead or alive, were seen. The continuous friendly casualties plus the impossibility of spotting visible foes caused morale to suffer, but the assault resolutely continued through the 18th and 19th.

On the 20th a ceasefire was declared from 0001 to 0730 hours, and an intense psychological operations campaign was launched, inviting enemy troops to either rally or surrender. At 0730 the attack resumed under a barrage of artillery and air strikes. The 5th MSF advanced and captured several caves and large ravines over the next two days. On the 22nd an extensive cave complex was uncovered. The next day a hospital complex was found. At 1825 hours on the 23rd a three-man patrol returned to friendly lines after one of the most daring escapades of the battle. These three strikers had traveled 300m underground and forward of friendly positions. They found several large caverns and three chambers filled with weapons. They had watched as approximately 100 male and female VC made final preparations to abandon Nui Coto. During the patrol the three killed seven VC. While returning they were challenged by VC guards at a cave entrance. They held up recovered AK-47s as a sign of identification and bluffed their way past. More caves and caches of enemy material and documents were uncovered on the 24th and 25th.

Intelligence from the defectors and the three-man patrol's report indicated the 5th MSF was now approaching the main enemy complex where the legendary VC leader, a Cambodian named Chau Kim, had his headquarters. His Cambodian ancestry gave him influence among the people in the Seven Sisters Mountains area. His defeat would severely damage VC prestige in this important portion of the delta. On the 26th the two battalions located the main cave. Most of the enemy had managed to slip away but almost 200 weapons and thousands of pages of documents, films, and records were captured. Numerous subsidiary caves were explored and much equipment uncovered.

Operations would continue until April 8 as the 5th MSF, assisted by other CIDG elements, mopped up enemy remnants. More caves and caches would be revealed on the other peaks around Nui Coto. After 20 years of enemy domination, the impregnable Tuk Chup Knoll had fallen. The VC boast of invincibility had been destroyed by the aggressiveness of the 4th and 5th MSF. There was still much to be accomplished in the pacification process, but a major step forward had been taken in demonstrating to the people that they no longer need fear the VC.

The flight route from Nha Trang to Bunard, Operation HARVEST MOON, April 2, 1967. The eight C-123 Provider transports of the 14th Air Commando Wing departed Long Van Airbase, Nha Trang at 0825 hours to fly out over the South China Sea as part of the deception plan and the 700ft drop was made on to Drop Zone Bellmont at 0930 hours. The pathfinders had been parachute inserted by a CH-47 helicopter.

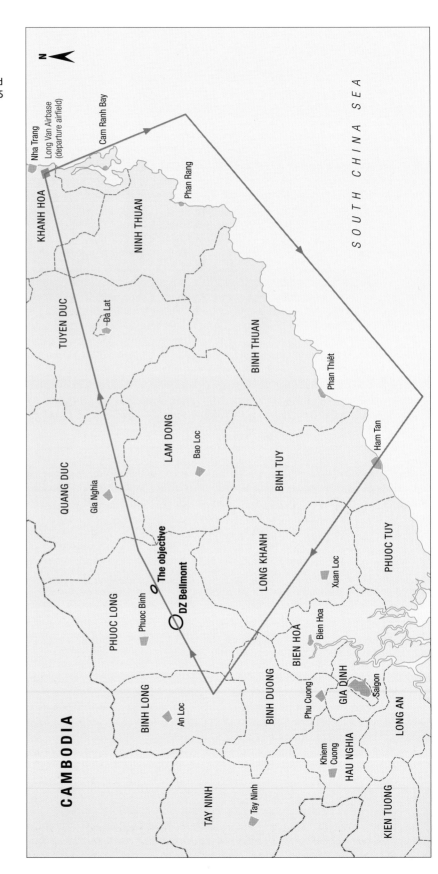

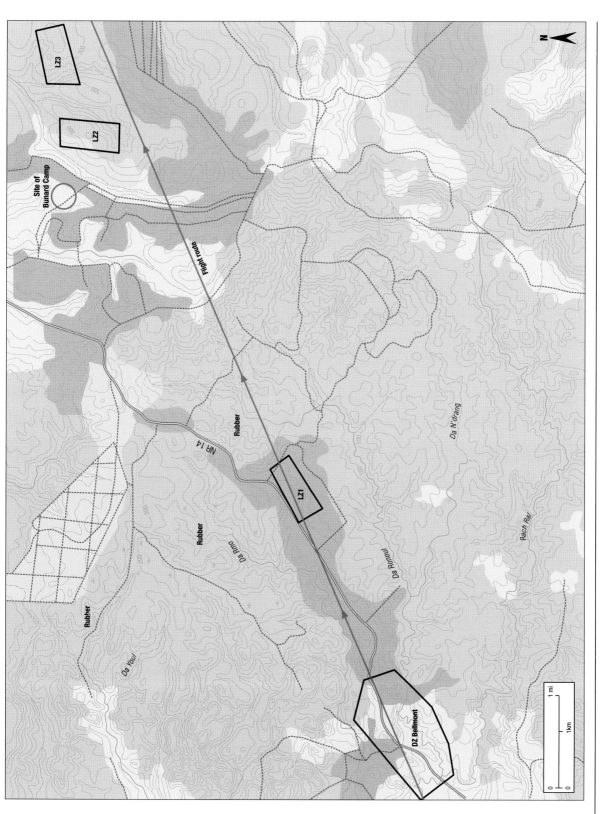

5th MIKE Force, Operation HARVEST MOON, April 2, 1967. The vegetation on the drop zone was 10–50ft high. The ground engagements were light and the paratroopers moved along the partly overgrown National Route 14 to secure the objective. The three landing zones were for troops and resupply helicopters. The future site of Camp Bunard is indicated near LZ 2.

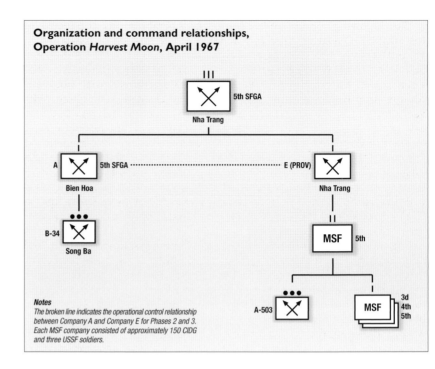

Organization and command relationships, Operation *Harvest Moon*, April 1967

III
5th SFGA
Nha Trang

A 5th SFGA ···················· E (PROV)
Bien Hoa
Nha Trang

B-34
Song Ba

II
MSF 5th

A-503
MSF
3d
4th
5th

Notes
The broken line indicates the operational control relationship between Company A and Company E for Phases 2 and 3. Each MSF company consisted of approximately 150 CIDG and three USSF soldiers.

The two MIKE Forces lost 45 dead and 191 wounded while the supporting CSFs lost nine dead and 14 wounded. There were three USSF killed and 24 wounded along with three dead LLDB and eight wounded. VC losses were 53 confirmed dead, ten captured, and 23 defected. Scores more were believed dead in the caves. Over 500 small arms, 13 crew-served weapons, large quantities of munitions, and 90,000 pages of documents were captured.

MIKE Force airborne operations

The MIKE Forces were to be airborne qualified to allow rapid insertion by parachute to reinforce camps, secure future camp sites, or block enemy withdrawal routes. Owing to attrition, not all companies were able to maintain parachute qualification. With the availability and capabilities of helicopters, parachute assaults were seldom executed. Only four such operations were conducted, dropping two or three companies. Admittedly, more USSF participated in these jumps than normally accompanied the MSF companies, but among these were command and control personnel and specialists to support the operation on the ground.[14]

On April 2, 1967 the 5th MSF conducted Operation HARVEST MOON, 35 miles northwest of Nha Trang. Their mission was to secure a site for the future Bunard Strike Force Camp on an infiltration trail in northeast III CTZ. It also tested the concept of a minimally trained MIKE Force's ability to conduct a parachute assault, assemble, and accomplish its combat mission. Task Force BLUE included A-503, a command and control element of Company E (Provisional), 5th SFGA; USSF medical element, 2d and 3d Companies, 5th MSF; and its Reconnaissance Platoon. Eighteen USSF pathfinders were first dropped by a CH-47. Eight C-123 transports dropped 350 strikers, 29 USSF, and three LLDB onto dry rice paddies 10km southwest of the camp site and were immediately engaged. There were several jump injuries, one MSF was killed in action and six wounded. The area was successfully cleared and camp construction soon began with additional MIKE Force units helicoptered in for security.

---

14 USSF participants were not eligible for the parachute assault star affixed to jumpwings (which was not official at the time), but in most cases received the Air Medal. They have not since been authorized the Combat Jump Bronze Star Device.

The following month another airborne operation was conducted by the 5th MSF. Operation BLACKJACK 41C had the mission of harassing the VC in the Seven Sisters Mountains. The battalion-sized IV CTZ MIKE Force had been operating there since April 20, 1967. On May 9 information was received that a VC company was preparing to defend Nui Giai Mountain. An operation would be launched on May 13 to clear the stronghold. With very short notice the 5th MSFC was ordered to parachute-deliver a battalion east of the mountain. The force included A-503, a command and control element of Company E (Provisional), 5th SFGA; USSF medical element, 3d, 4th and 5th Companies, 5th MSF; and its Mortar Platoon. MGF 399 established a blocking position on the southeast tip of Nui Giai while three CSF companies from Vinh Gia (LLDB A-149 – an LLDB-operated camp without a USSF A-team; there were only about one or two such camps per CTZ) – Ba Xoai (A-421), and Tinh Bien (A-423) set up blocking positions to the north and west.

The airborne force of 374 strikers and 20 USSF jumped from C-130s at 0645 hours on May 13 east of the mountain and moved up its slopes in an attempt to drive the VC into the blocking positions. There were simply too many places for the enemy to hide and they used the caves to move from one position to another. Contacts were made every day except the 15th. On the 16th the blocking elements began thrusts on to the mountain. The IV CTZ MIKE Force was withdrawn on the 16th and the operation was terminated on the 18th as it was apparent the VC could not be flushed out. Two CSF companies remained to harass the enemy. Forty VC were known to have been killed. Friendly losses were nine dead and 25 wounded.

On October 1, 1967 Camp Lac Thien in II CTZ was converted to Regional Force and its A-team was assigned to open a new camp at Bu Prang 45 miles southwest of Ban Me Thuot near the Cambodian border. To secure the construction site the II CTZ MIKE Force would jump in two companies on October 5, in Operation BLUE MAX. A provisional pathfinder force of 11 USSF and 37 MSF jumped in to secure and mark the drop zone. They were soon followed by Task Force ALPHA with A-217, C-2 command and control element, support personnel, and the 24th and 25th Companies, II CTZ MSF with 50 USSF and 275 MSF, which included a number of LLDB, jumping from six C-130s. There was no enemy resistance and the site was secured. A-236 and two companies from the former Luc Thien Camp (Task Force BRAVO) were helicoptered in, took over site security, and commenced camp construction. The MSF companies patrolled the surrounding area. In late November an overland convoy with engineers, construction materials, and supplies reached Bu Prang. The camp later proved effective in hindering NVA infiltration.

In November 1968 the most ambitious effort to take the Seven Sisters Mountains was executed involving two MIKE Force battalions, five ARVN Ranger battalions, and other units. Operation SEVEN MOUNTAINS would be led off by a 5th MSF airborne assault on November 17. A pathfinder element from C-4 was landed by helicopter to secure the drop zone east of the mountains. Thirty minutes later Task Force ALPHA with A-503, a C-4 command and control element, support personnel, and the 2d, 3d and 5th Companies, 5th MSF jumped in from ten C-130s: 495 strikers and 25 USSF in total. Once they reached their phase lines the Ranger battalions, part of Task Force Ranger, began helicoptering into LZs to the south and advanced on the mountain along with the 5th MSF. The 4th MSF, Task Force BRAVO, was lifted in after the Rangers from Ba Xoai, the operation's FOB. Three batteries of 105mm and two of 155mm howitzers provided fire support. Two Ranger battalions were on two-hour standby alert at Ba Xoai to be airmobiled in if necessary and two CSF companies at Ba Xoai (A-421) and one at Vinh Gia (LLDB A-149) were on six-hour alert. The action was continuous and led to a follow-on series of operations to clear the Seven Sisters Mountains into 1969.

Operation SEVEN MOUNTAINS task organization, November 1968
Command and Control Element, C-4 (Co D, 5th SFGA)
Task Force ALPHA (5th MSFC)
5th MSFC Command Group (less elements)
2d MSF Company
3d MSF Company
5th MSF Company
Task Force BRAVO (4th MSFC)
4th MSFC Command Group (less elements)
43d MSF Company
44th MSF Company
45th MSF Company
47th MSF Company
Task Force RANGER
4th Ranger Group Headquarters
32d Ranger Battalion
41st Ranger Battalion
42d Ranger Battalion
43d Ranger Battalion
44th Ranger Battalion
6th Battalion (105mm), 77th Artillery
Platoon, Battery H (Searchlight), 29th Artillery
Support Task Force
164th Aviation Group elements, 13th and 307th Aviation Battalions
Psychological Warfare Team
Aid Station
Signal Company
Medical Ambulance Company
Aerial Port Detachment (USAF)

An assessment of MIKE Forces

The MIKE Forces can be considered a reasonably successful counterinsurgency effort in spite of their numerous limitations and shortcomings, which can be summarized as follows:

- Lightly armed and equipped.
- Limited tactical mobility.
- Limited level of individual and unit training.
- Limited logistical sustainment capabilities.
- Low troop education level with a low percentage of literacy.
- Elected or appointed leaders with little, if any, formal training.
- Consisted of disenfranchised ethnic minorities with political agendas differing from those of the Vietnamese government.
- Lack of a military judicial system.
- Able to resign when desired.
- Marginal levels of military discipline.

In many circumstances the MIKE Force concept as conducted in Vietnam would not have worked. The reasons for its success lay in the US Special Forces. It was a concept in which they believed and which they made work through their own dedication and initiative. They went to great lengths to motivate and develop the strikers and their leadership. They cultivated respect from the strikers, gaining their loyalty through fair treatment. The strikers tended to fight for their comrades and the Americans who supported them and not necessarily the Vietnamese government, but they did oppose the common enemy. Regardless of the nominal command of the MIKE Forces by the LLDB, it was the USSF that controlled the pay, rations, supplies, equipment, and operational funds. This provided a degree of control over the LLDB, preventing corruption and the siphoning of funds and resources.

The most serious hindrance experienced by the MIKE Forces came in the form of the LLDB. One USSF major, an MSFC XO, summed it up in a statement to an Army historical team interviewer:

> The LLDB are not capable of commanding these organizations. They would find it difficult to maintain the present posture, to say the least, or anything approaching it. I think our mission and the role of the 4th MSF are being disrupted by the presence of the LLDB. The total effort here should be preparing the indigenous leaders in the companies and battalions to take over; we should be training battalion staffs. Then the whole organization should be turned over to a particular district or province as Regional Forces. I have never really understood why the LLDB were placed in the program. They add nothing. They're simply another organization that has to be tied in and coordinated with. In most instances it completely confuses the issue when we are working directly … which we generally do here … with indigenous troops. The utilization of the LLDB in this organization has come to naught.

There were effective LLDB personnel, mostly NCOs, but overall they only provided another layer of decision making (or rather, indecision) placed corrupt LLDB in a position to exploit the CIDG, and made the situation more complex by having to accommodate an organization that contributed little and was mistrusted by the strikers. It would have been far more effective for the USSF to have trained and developed indigenous leadership within the MSF and mentored them to eventually take over. The effort would have been much better served if CIDG platoon, company, and battalion leadership development courses had been implemented.

The five MIKE Forces conducted thousands of offensive, search and clear, patrol, raid, camp reinforcement, reaction force, reconnaissance-in-force, and mobile guerrilla operations from platoon to multi-battalion in size. They suffered occasional defeats, but for the most part the operations were successful. The MIKE Force effort fielded five brigade-size light infantry forces requiring relatively little support. Training, basing, and logistical support were limited, as were the pay and maintenance costs. Fewer than 500 USSF led and advised the MIKE Forces of almost 11,000 strikers at their peak. The 5th SFGA Logistical Support Center in Nha Trang and its C-team branches were manned by only 250 US soldiers and a few hundred indigenous civilians, who not only supported the MIKE Forces, but all of the scores of other CIDG operations. For what the MIKE Forces provided in combat capabilities, their cost was little compared to US and even ARVN forces.

As with MIKE Forces, no organizations parallel to the Vietnam reconnaissance projects have since been formed. The techniques developed by the projects have long been studied and are still valid and adapted by current special operations forces. They provided invaluable intelligence to MACV and other commands. Up to 50 percent of intelligence on enemy troop locations and logistical activities received by MACV was provided by Special Forces.

Stand-down

All along, the plan was for the USSF to "work themselves out of a job." It is seldom that a military organization being relieved has to plan for, train, and provide its replacement organization, but that is what the 5th SFGA did. Strike Force camps in pacified areas were closed, and through 1970 other camps were converted to Regional Forces or to Border Ranger battalions. The MIKE Forces were reduced in size, with the strikers given options. They could transfer to understrength CSFs for conversion to Regional Forces or Border Rangers; they could resign; or they could remain in their units, which would be broken up and converted to Regional Forces (or Border Rangers in the case of the I CTZ MSF) and reassigned to new locations. Those wishing to resign, but deemed "draft dodgers," were informed they would be drafted into the ARVN. The USSF and LLDB initiated a motivation and indoctrination program promoting the benefits of conversion to ARVN, one of which was that minorities would receive full Vietnamese citizenship. The large civilian work force had to be given their severance, and efforts were made to find them employment. The USSF teams were inactivated in-country as their CIDG units were closed or converted and the 5th SFGA colors were returned to Ft Bragg, NC on March 3, 1971. The CIDG program was terminated on December 31, 1970 and the Recondo School closed its doors on December 19. The LLDB, most of whom were absorbed into the Regional Forces or Border Rangers to assume command, was dissolved the next day. The best of the LLDB were reassigned to the Strategic Technical Directorate, a special reconnaissance operation taking over from MACV-SOG.

The US has not since raised a MIKE Force-like organization in any of the many conflicts it has been involved with. Instead, Special Forces are employed as trainers for indigenous paramilitary and irregular forces under their own, often politically appointed, leadership – resulting in the traditional problems of corruption, ineffectiveness, and mis-utilization. It is an option that might be reviewed and considered for implementation in future conflicts.

Bibliography

Burruss, L. H. *MIKE Force* (New York: Pocket Books, 1989).

Donahue, James C. *Blackjack-33: With Special Forces in the Viet Cong Forbidden Zone* (Novato, CA: Presidio Press, 1999).

Donahue, James C. *Blackjack-34* – previously published as *No Greater Love* (New York: Ballantine Books, 1988/2000).

Donahue, James C. *Mobile Guerrilla Force: With the Special Forces in War Zone D* (Annapolis, MD: Naval Institute Press, 1996).

Kelly, Francis J. *US Army Special Forces, 1961–1971.* Vietnam Studies series. (Washington, DC: Department of the Army, 1973).

Simpson, Charles M. *Inside the Green Berets* (Novato, CA: Presidio Press, 1983).

Stanton, Shelby *Green Berets at War: US Army Special Forces in Southeast Asia 1956–1975* (Novato, CA: Presidio Press, 1985).

Stanton, Shelby *Special Forces at War: An Illustrated History, Southeast Asia 1957–1975* (Charlottesville, VA: Howell Press, 1990).

Stanton, Shelby *Vietnam Order of Battle: A Complete Illustrated Reference to U.S. Army Combat and Support Forces in Vietnam 1961–1973* (Mechanicsburg, PA: Stackpole Books, 2003).

The Green Beret Magazine (5th SFGA monthly publication, 1966–70). Vol. I–V. Complete reprint set available from RADIX Associates, 2314 Cheshire Ln., Houston, TX 77018-4023, USA.

Additional details on USSF, the LLDB, and Special Forces camps can be found in the following Osprey Publishing titles, written by the same author:

Elite 4: *US Special Forces 1952–84.*
Elite 29: *Vietnam Airborne.*
Warrior 28: *Green Beret in Vietnam 1957–73.*
Fortress 33: *Special Forces Camps in Vietnam 1961–70.*

Abbreviations

AATTV	Australian Army Training Team, Vietnam	MIKE	Mobile Strike
AO	area of operations	MSF	Mobile Strike Force
ARVN	Army of the Republic of Vietnam (pronounced "are-vin")	MSFC	Mobile Strike Force Command
		MSS	Mission Support Site
ASA	Army Security Agency	NCO	non-commissioned officer
BAR	Browning automatic rifle	NVA	North Vietnamese Army
BDA	Bomb damage assessment	OPCON	operational control
CIDG	Civilian Irregular Defense Group (pronounced "sidge")	RT	reconnaissance team
		PRU	provisional reconnaissance unit
CLD	Command Liaison Detachment	PZ	pick-up zone
CRP	combat reconnaissance platoon	RON	remain over night (position)
CSF	Camp Strike Force	RTO	radio-telephone operator
CTZ	Corps tactical zone	SFGA	Special Forces Group (Airborne)
Det	Detachment	SFOB	Special Forces operational base
FFV	Field Force, Vietnam	SFOD	Special Forces operational detachment
FOB	forward operating base	SOD	Special operations detachment
HEAT	High-explosive antitank	SWA	Special weapons augmentation platoon
HQ	Headquarters	TAOR	Tactical area of responsibility
LAW	Light antitank weapon	TDY	temporary duty
LLDB	Nhay-Du Luc-Luong Dac-Biet (Airborne Special Forces Command)	TOE	Table of Organization and Equipment
		USARV	US Army, Vietnam
LRP	Long range patrol	USSF	United States Special Forces
LZ	Landing zone	VC	Viet Cong
MACV	Military Assistance Command, Vietnam	WO	warrant officer (Australian senior NCO)
MACV-SOG	MACV-Studies and Observation Group		
MG	machine gun	WP	White phosphorous
MGF	Mobile Guerrilla Force	XO	executive officer (second-in-command)

Index